A Boy, A Ball, And A Dream:

The Marvin Wood Story

Kerry D. Marshall

Scott Publications
Indianapolis

Scott Publications
First Trade Edition   August 1991

Cover design, illustrations and layout, were provided by George Murff and Universal Graphics.

Library of Congress Catalog Number: 91-617c7

ISBN 0-9630362-0-3 (Hardbound)
    0-9630362-1-1 (Paperback)

Manufactured in the United States of America

Acknowledgements

This book is dedicated to anyone who has ever had occasion to be the "underdog."

Writing this biography would not have been possible without the held of many people. At the risk of leaving someone out, I list them here: Thank you to John Shaughnessy, Victor Mukes, Eileen Wood, Vera and Jerry Lain, Mike Chapman, Herb Scwomeyer, Bobby Plump, Ray Craft, Gene White, Rollin Cutter, Bob Engel, Bob Williams, Bob Collins, Gerl Furr, Wendell Trogdon, Bob Wiles, Walter O'Brien, Jimmy Doyle, Marvin Cave, Lowell Boring, Mike Needham, Don Cromer, Jo-Ann Nester, The ladies of St. Mary's 1990-91 basketball team, Tim Kizer, Audie Freeman, Max Eby, Ralph Causey, Robert Smith, Glen "Lefty" Jacobs, Jack Beatty, Jay McCreary, Marc Combs, Barter and Betty Dobson, Genevieve White, Harold McWilliams, John Wood, Wayne and Martha Wood, Bob Tanguy, "Ike" Tallman, Cale Hudson, Joe Wolfla, George Murff, Kathy McQueen and Rosy McKittrick.

A special thanks to my wife Rebecca who helped to make my dream come true.

Introduction

I first met Marvin Wood when I was twelve. My teammates and I had just lost the final game of Mishawaka's elementary basketball tournament. I was as disappointed as a twelve-year-old could be and accepted my second-place ribbon with teary eyes. After receiving my award I heard a voice say to us: "Boys, don't be too upset, if you work real hard maybe by the time you get to the high school we can win one of these." I turned to the voice and saw a man pointing to a piece of jewelry on his finger. The man was Marvin Wood and the jewelry was a gold state championship ring.

Years later, Marvin Wood gave me the most devastating news of my childhood—He cut me from his high school basketball team. As coach Wood explained that I was neither quick enough nor tall enough to continue to compete, I resolved that I would find some other area in which I could excel. This will to make such a resolution came, in part, from learning about success and failure as a member of basketball teams.

I graduated from high school, went to college, and if I had any success at all it was due in part to the discipline and "never-say-die" attitude I'd learned from playing basketball. A phrase I'd heard coach Wood use in summer camps became especially important to me. "Boys," he'd say, "luck is what happens when opportunity meets preparation."

In 1987 "Hoosiers," a movie based on the '54 Milan team Marvin coached to the state championship, gained national recognition. Remembering good-hearted Marvin and the look that came to his eyes whenever Milan was mentioned made me eager to see the film. I enjoyed the movie, but came away feeling that Hollywood had missed the mark as to the true meaning of the title, "Hoosiers." I'd been associated with Marvin during some difficult years—during years when the last shots did not go in, when the breaks were not going his way, and when the talent was not as deep. Yet, I could not imagine the players from the championship team having a different impression of Marvin than those of us who knew him when things were not going quite as well.

Thousands of young men and women annually compete for the opportunity to win a state championship—few find themselves both prepared and lucky enough to win. However, everyone who tries finds in basketball a classroom where the coach is a teacher who provides his or her pupils a chance to learn about success, failure, and the discipline required to handle the joy and sorrow that accompanies competition. These lessons are not lost once the playing days are over. This is why the game and those who teach and play it are so important to our state. "Hoosier Hysteria" is part of the foundation from which our culture is built and dedicated coaches such as Marvin Wood are the pillars of that foundation.

Kerry D. Marshall   March, 1991

Contents

"It's nice to be important, but it's more important to be nice."

Mary Lou Wood, 1954 -

The Indiana State High School Basketball Tournament, one of the top sporting events in the country, has been the forum for many of our state's most treasured moments. The tournament features some of the best basketball players in the nation and has been a "proving ground" for coaches employing a wide variety of strategies for victory. The event's attraction is found in the ideal that, no matter how big or small, no matter what the odds might be, every school has a chance to win. And for every team taking the court as an underdog there is a beacon from the past, a legend to give them the hope and courage to overcome the odds. The legend is known as the "Milan Miracle."

Twenty-six-year-old Marvin Wood, former farm boy, Butler University graduate, and Tony Hinkle protege, huddled his Milan Indians around him. He and his players were eighteen seconds away from upsetting mighty Muncie Central for the 1954 Indiana State Basketball Championship. In the stands behind the bench and all around the Butler Fieldhouse court, 14,943 fans screamed their hearts out. Despite the tremendous pressure of the moment, Marvin calmly gave his lads instructions. Down the floor the Muncie Central Bearcats consulted with their coach. The heat of the moment showed in their faces as they hung on his every word. Muncie had been picked to win this game. But now, with the score tied and the clock ticking down, their opponents had the ball and two of the slickest guards in the state. The outcome of this game was now a matter of no small debate—A debate ringing throughout every nook and cranny in the arena and in nearly every living room in the state.

Many fans had hoped for this scenario. Muncie Central, the state's perennial basketball powerhouse, was the solid favorite. Milan had not been expected to get past Terre Haute Gerstmeyer, their opponent in the afternoon's semi-final. The fact that tiny Milan High had gotten this far at all seemed unlikely. The school had only 161 students, the town 1,150 citizens. Such a small school had never won a state basketball championship—unless you count Thorntown which won in 1915, but that was two wars and nearly forty years ago. Even the most optimistic observer had to concede that Milan, whose tallest player was barely over six feet, would have slim chances at beating a team with taller and quicker players.

When the claxon blared and the two teams converged on the shiny wooden floor. The crowd re-doubled their voices which threatened to lift the roof of the cavernous gym. At the heighth of this din, Bobby Plump, the Indian's sensational senior guard, triggered the ball into play. Plump, who earlier had calmly held the ball at half-court for nearly four-and-a-half minutes while his team was trailing, dribbled to his right while his teammates: Ronald Truitt, Rollin Cutter, Raymond Craft, and Gene White, formed a line on the left sideline. Plump's defender warily placed himself between Bob and the basket while the other Bearcats kept a comfortable distance between the line of Indians. The clock wound down to eight seconds. Plump quickened his dribble, faked left, and then drew hard back to the right in a line for the basket. At the four second mark he stopped, drew a bead on the basket, and lofted a jumpshot. When the ball deflected against the back of the rim and sagged safely into the net, the crowd exploded from their seats and acted like crazy people.

Plump and his teammates, coached well enough to know that three seconds was world enough and time for their opponent to score, found their men and assumed defense positions. Their opponents failed to mount an attack. The claxon gave its final blare announcing the end of the game and the beginning of a legend.

1

Childhood on the Family Farm

Marvin's second grade photo.

The life of Marvin Wood is a success story. His story, abetted by the hand of fate, is planted firmly in a foundation of hard work, team play, and faith—seeds planted during his childhood.

Born on 21 January 1928, Marvin Carroll Wood was the first of four sons blessed to Carroll and Iris Wood. The Woods lived on a farm south of the central Indiana hamlet of Fountaintown where Carroll farmed and worked on a milk route. Marvin's grandparents, the Woods and the Borings, lived within a few miles of their children and most of his other relatives resided "within a stone's throw."

Marvin, raised with a great deal of love and attention from this extended family, readily admits he would not have been able to accomplish what he has without the love and devotion of his family to whom he gives credit for his spiritual and moral foundation. "When I was a child I received a lot of encouragement from adults," he recalls. "They taught me to believe in myself and as I grew up there was never a doubt in my mind that I could become whatever I wanted to be."

Life on the family farm during the 1930s was different from life on the farm today. Most farms lacked indoor plumbing and electricity. In general, farm families earned little money and could not afford more than one set of "Sunday-go-to meetin'" clothes for each member of the household. A well-worn pair of bibbed overalls and a half-dozen or so T-shirts completed a farmer's wardrobe. Out in the fields the horse and plough tilled the soil at a snail's pace. The most handy set of tools was often a pair of calloused hands. In short, a living earned from the soil did not come without steel-willed dedication and buckets of perspiration.

The Great Depression presented an added burden to farmers because little capital was available for expansion and modernization. Dust storms and drought ravaged the Middle West which further tested the farm community and made cooperation between farmers essential for survival. Farm families often made sacrifices so their relatives and neighbors could survive. Growing up in such an environment taught young Marvin the value of teamwork. "We worked together on the farm as a team and it always made me feel good to know that I'd done my part to help. There were many occasions when my father sent my brothers and me to help a neighbor who had fallen on hard times. Some of my fondest childhood memories involve working with friends to help some one in need. I enjoyed being able to help other folks and they always let me know that they appreciated my help. I also liked the praise I received for doing a good work. So when I was assigned a job—even some menial chore such as sweeping the barn floor—I tried to do it well."

The Wood boys learned to farm with the help of a hired hand, Art House. Art taught the boys how to do their various chores in an efficient and safe manner. Marvin is still impressed with the patience and thoughtfulness of their older, handicapped teacher. Art's ability to do a good job, despite his disabilities, showed the boys how hard work and a good attitude can overcome almost any obstacle.

"My dad used Art twofold," recalls Marvin. "Art did the chores around the farm and he'd take us around with him. He taught us how to harness the horse and showed us the quickest way to husk corn (both hands at the top and pull down). Art's handicaps made him slow and methodical. He was a patient man and with patience he taught us how to be safe and efficient young farmers.

"When I think of Art I can't help but be reminded of his old Model T Ford. We begged him to teach us how to drive it and after hounding him for months he finally did. We nearly scared him to death a few times during those driving lessons. Teaching driver's education gave me a greater appreciation of what it must have been like for Art to sit in the passenger seat while I learned to drive."

While Art gave the boys an education in farming (and driving), Marvin's uncle Harold taught the Wood boys the rudiments of business. Marvin recalls his uncle's instructions to be polite to customers on the milk route and to be attentive to the small details such as closing gates or thanking folks for their business. Harold also taught Marvin how to determine a fair price for his labor and how to collect delinquent accounts without insulting the delinquent party.

"My uncle Harold was a no-nonsense businessman who believed in a fair wage for a day's work," says Marvin. "He had little tolerance for sloughfulness. I remember once we had a neighbor boy helping us with the milk route and sometimes he'd come in about twenty minutes late. This happened two or three times and then one day we just up and left without him. The boy was about a quarter of a mile away from the house so we could see him walking down the road, but when Harold said we were leaving at six-thirty he meant it."

Summer mornings for Marvin began at four-thirty a.m. when he'd arise to milk the cows, feed the chickens, and slop the hogs. His mother served breakfast at six. The family ate breakfast and all of their meals together. After breakfast the boys would either head out for a day on the milk route or a day in the fields. When they'd completed their chores young Marvin and his brothers found plenty of time for other pursuits such as swimming, softball, boxing and, of course, basketball.

With the day's work under their belts and out of their minds, the boys scrambled around the barnyard chasing a battered softball, or pitching baskets at a rusty rim perched on the side of the barn. The three oldest boys, Marvin, Wayne and John developed their skills by competing with each other. They received additional coaching from their father and their uncle Lowell.

Lowell came around once a day to collect milk. Whenever he had time he gave the boys a few pointers. He taught them how to pivot on one foot, how to use a head fake and cross step, how to shoot both a two-handed set shot and a one-hand jumpshot. Lowell was the first family member Marvin saw compete in an organized game. In 1939 his folks took him to Shelbyville to watch Lowell play in the sectional. The experience left Marvin yearning for the opportunity to play in a sectional too. His desire coupled with coaching from his uncles and father helped Marvin develop the skills that would make him a tough competitor both on and off the basketball court.

With work and play came the inevitable lessons in life—lessons about honesty and the consequences for foolish behavior. In a speech given for the Morristown Chamber of Commerce in the Spring of 1990, Marvin recalled one such lesson: "My grandmother was a sweet, dear old lady. She thought I was a little angel and she treated me with lots of love. I was in her house alone one day. I must have been about five or six at the time. She had an old Victrola in which she kept a jar of quarters. I was old enough to understand the value of money and I needed some cash for a little candy or something, so I opened that old Victrola and swiped a quarter.

"When I got home from grandmother's that day my mother was in the yard getting ready to do the wash. She took one look at my dirty jeans and demanded that I immediately take them off so she could wash them. Knowing that she would find the quarter in my pocket, I hemmed and hawed about giving her the pants until she nearly took them off me herself. Needless to say, she found the quarter and questioned me as to where I'd gotten it. I told her what I'd done and after she'd given me a whipping she told me to take the money back to grandma. I think I would have rather had another whipping than to face my grandmother and tell her I'd stolen a quarter from her. It was one of the hardest things I ever did.

"My grandmother forgave me, but as I walked along the road back home I cried a little because I knew that my halo had been tarnished quite a bit. That little episode taught me a valuable lesson: It takes a long time to earn a good reputation, but it only takes a few minutes to ruin it."

In another incident Marvin and his brothers, Wayne and John, snuck out to the barn with a pack of cigarettes and some matches. Up in the hay loft they were about to take a drag on their first cigarette when the match tumbled from Marvin's hand into the hay below. In no time at all the barn was engulfed by flames and the three boys narrowly escaped with their lives. The fire destroyed the barn and their uncle Harold's new car.

Cowering at the feet of their elders, the three young lads awaited retribution, but as they listened to the grown-ups discuss the mishap one of the neighbors hypothesized that the freshly-mown hay had set itself afire. He called it "spontaneous combustion" and everyone, including three guilty-but-relieved boys agreed. Wayne, John and Marvin realized this act of foolishness had brought them close to death. And even though they were not held responsible, they learned that negligence can lead to danger and destruction. (Incidently, the boys eventually fessed-up to starting that fire. They told their father about it in 1964.)

Aside from work and play, Marvin had school to attend. His mother, Iris, had been a good student in high school and she understood that her sons would need a solid education to help them face the challenges of a fast-changing world. With this in mind, she made certain that her boys found a proper balance between farming, schooling, and playing. Marvin's parents were supported in their efforts by the rest of the family and the community. "We were surrounded by good people who were concerned about our development," says Marvin. "That really made a difference in us and was probably one of the main reasons why I got into education and coaching."

He cites Nathan Moore, his teacher for grades five through

eight, as the first in a series of excellent educators who made a lasting impression on him. When asked about Mr. Moore, Marvin's face brightens up. "Nathan Moore, what a jewel! He was the first male teacher I had. A big guy, about 6'1" or so, he'd been a great athlete in high school. Mr. Moore was a powerful force in our community. He taught children during the week and adults on Sunday in church. By being big, soft spoken, and pleasant he earned respect. What really impressed me about him was the amount of time he gave to each of us children.

"I remember the first student in our school with a 'learning disability.' Mr. Moore spent a lot of time and energy encouraging that young man to learn. This six-footer was down on his knees beside the boy's desk for hours at a spell. With patience he encouraged learning." Marvin ran into that student at a Sears store many years later. The gentleman was a department manager. "He had that job because Mr. Moore believed in a struggling child's abilities even when the boy may not have believed in himself," explains Marvin. "The line: 'No man stands as tall as when he stoops to help a child' certainly applies to Nathan Moore. He was an excellent role model."

Marvin attended school in a two-room schoolhouse with twenty-four other students. He feels that he had advantages over children who were educated under different circumstances. "Our school was like one big family. If someone in my class had a problem, then we all had a problem. If one person had trouble learning math, then we all had to pitch in and help that person learn."

Attending such a small school also taught Marvin some interesting lessons about social relationships. "We played softball and our class was so small that everyone played— including the girls. We had no idea that girls weren't supposed to play ball with boys until we went to play another elementary school. They laughed at us because we were playing with girls— but they didn't laugh for long. We had a girl named Imogene. She was probably the best softball player in the county. She and the other gals could pitch, hit and run as good, or better, than most of the guys. Our teams played great ball and we did not lose many games. We appreciated the talent the girls brought to our teams. In fact, without them we had no team.

"I was also very fortunate to have a black young man, Sylvester Blythe, as a classmate and friend. By having Sylvester as a classmate, we did not learn prejudice. Instead we had a friend who was different from the rest of us—the biggest difference had nothing to do with color. Sylvester had come from the big city (Indianapolis) and didn't know much about farming. We learned about Indianapolis from him and he learned about farming from us.

"He moved to Fountaintown to live with his grandparents and he often came by our house to play. I remember he used to hold out his hand when you offered him a piece of candy. We just stuck our hands in the bag and grabbed a handful, but Sylvester had been taught to hold out his hand and wait to have the candy given to him. That always struck me as being a little strange, but after I got a little older and saw some of the things that went on between the races I understood.

"In the country we saw things differently—a strong mind and back were valuable so we had little concern about the color of the calloused hands next to us in the milk shed or in the fields. I remember the first time someone made fun of Sylvester for being black. A new kid had come to our school and on his first day we let him be a captain of our softball game at recess. Well, the first thing out of his mouth when we were choosing sides was: 'I'll take blackie.' Boy, that shocked us! We'd never heard anyone be disrespectful on account of the color of someone's skin. Sylvester handled it well. He simply went over to this kid who was about six inches shorter than him and calmly said: 'That'll be enough of that.' The boy looked back at us and when he saw none of us were smiling it pretty much put an end to that.

"We all felt fortunate to have big ole' Sylvester as a friend and classmate. In fact, Sylvester was instrumental in getting me involved in organized basketball. One day he went to Mr. Moore and asked him if we could have a team. Moore agreed and by the time I was in eighth grade we won the county tournament."

While Marvin enjoyed other sports, his first love would always be basketball. By the time he got into the eighth grade, his skills as a basketball player had developed to the point where opposing teams had to key on stopping him, or risk the chance of being run out of the gym by a five-foot-six-inch fireball. The annual contest between Morristown and Fountain-town provided an example of his growing prowess. Morristown had developed a special defense to stop Marvin from scoring.

Even so, the Morristown quintet lost to Fountaintown 17-16. The low-scoring game would tend to indicate their defensive scheme had nearly worked—except for the fact that every one of Fountaintown's points came from little Marvin Wood!

Marvin's Sixth Grade Class Photo from Fountaintown Elementary (Marvin is in the second row, sixth from the left.)

While Marvin absorbed his studies and honed his athletic skills, his parents and the rest of the country struggled in the throes of the Great Depression. Marvin confesses that he and other people his age did not really understand what the Depression was until years later. "All I know is that everyone was poor. But we lived on a farm with livestock and a large garden, so we never went hungry. I suppose our wardrobes were somewhat limited. We had one pair of shoes and spent most of the summer running around in our bare feet. We had our Sunday best and a pair or two of overalls that mom was always mending. When I look back at those times I think the depression taught us to take care of things. We could not afford to waste anything and we learned the value of money and about how hard you have to work to earn it."

Time often tarnishes the reality of the way things once were. Such is the case for the perception of a family farm before the coming of electricity and indoor plumbing. Young Marvin studied his lessons and read books such as *Bears of Blue River* and *The Adventures of Huckleberry Finn* under the quavering light of a kerosene lamp. He recalls with mixed memories the many late-evening trudges to the out house with its snow-sifted seat. "Electricity and indoor plumbing completely changed our lives. I can remember when the electric poles were being placed along the road and how we kids would run off to watch each farm along the way have its electricity turned on. Electricity was a new, powerful tool and we were a little afraid of it. Nonetheless, once we had it we had plenty of light at night. We could refrigerate and freeze food and in the barn we had electrical appliances which made farming much more efficient."

Whatever the Woods lacked in material possessions was augmented by the bounties of nature found in and around the fertile plains running North and South of US 52. Driving East from Indianapolis or West from Rushville, the casual observer cannot help but to occasionally glance at the the heather-lined fields of green spreading for miles on either side of the two-lane highway. To this day, Fountaintown remains a rural haven. The town has but one church, a grain elevator, and several small stores.

Sugar Creek and Brandywine River bend and weave through these plains. Their sandy shoals create "beaches" and "swimming holes" where a hot summer afternoon might be passed in cool comfort. Wood fondly recalls a swimming hole not far from their farm. "We had a swimming hole on the Brandywine River about a half a mile from the farm. Some of us boys put up a sign Which read: 'Naked boys swim here every weekend.' There were about twenty of us who'd swim and bath down there. The river had a gentle current which kept the water fresh, clean, and cool. We didn't have running water until I was older, so on hot summer days the swimming hole was a great place to cool off and clean up for the evening meal."

In 1935 the Wood's fortunes took an unexpected upswing because of a general strike by milk truck drivers. As a result of that strike, Marvin's father, whose income depended on the proceeds from the milk he sold, found it necessary to deliver their milk directly to the dairy. It wasn't long before his neighbors asked him to help them get their milk to the dairy too. Before the strike ended, Carroll found he needed several trucks to meet the demands of the dairy farmers in his area. After the strike many of his temporary customers decided they preferred to have their milk picked up by someone who understood the dairy business from a farmer's perspective.

Thus, Carroll found himself in business.

"I suppose nowadays, the way unions run things, dad would probably face a lot of resistance in such an effort," admits Marvin. "But back then, all the farmers knew was that if the milk did not get to the dairy it would sour and they would be out money. Times were bad enough and dad was trying to do right by the neighbors. I think he was blessed because of it."

The milk route provided the Woods with extra money which allowed them to purchase a car and get the boys new shoes and additional clothing. "The milk route provided a new way of life for us," recalls Marvin. "We'd been living week-to-week and I know my parents had been much concerned about what the future might bring. The business gave them security and hope. It was an answer to my mother's prayers."

Iris Wood played an important role in Marvin's life. He gives her credit for helping him gain self-confidence and for leading him to a saving knowledge of Jesus Christ. Marvin's spiritual education began almost before he learned to walk. His grandmother Boring sang religious hymns as she worked. Not a timid lady, she felt inclined to sing her praises to God in clear tones that carried throughout the house and yard. Little Marvin heard these songs over and over. His mother, too, enjoyed to singing while she worked and, beyond that, she insisted the boys attend church and bible school.

Fountaintown Methodist, where the Wood family attended church, was the major social gathering place for most of the farm families in the area. The church provided a spiritual haven in which families could come and share their faith with their neighbors. The church also provided a social forum in which topics ranging from world wars to the birth of the community's newest member could be discussed.

Farming is a solitary life—especially once the schooling is out of the way. The church offered folks an opportunity to end a week of semi-solitude. Each Sunday farm families came to listen to the the preacher and to socialize with other farmers. Of course, their perspectives could not help but be influenced by their minister who exhorted them to live by faith.

Such a social orientation made a lasting impression on Marvin. He loved to go to church to hear about God and the world around them. "I learned a lot on Sunday mornings," he admits. "More importantly, I discovered at a young age that the word of God is powerful. I learned that faith can indeed move mountains." The church's elders were so impressed with Marvin's spiritual maturity they elected him as Sunday school superintendent at the tender age of seventeen.

His uncle Lowell, a church elder, remembered young Marvin this way: "I don't think Marvin was ever really a boy. He was as a little baby and then bang! He became a thoughtful little man who had all kinds of questions about how things were supposed to be. He seemed to grasp ideas well and we knew he'd become something in life. We were all proud when he was elected as Sunday School Superintendent. He could talk to grown-ups on their level and we could always count on him for good advice."

In summing up how much faith in God and living right had impressed him as a boy, Marvin recalls a humorous story he told his brother Keith: "When Keith asked me why I considered my faith in God to be so important. I told him: 'Keith, you know how every once in a while you put up a shot and it rolls around that old rim like it can't make up its mind to fall in or out? Well, I think that my faith in God helps maybe one or two out of ten of those shots to fall through.'" On a crisp March day in 1954 that faith would be put to the ultimate test.

2

Morristown High
1942-43

In the Fall of 1942, while his country struggled against aggressions around the globe, Marvin, armed with self confidence, boundless curiosity, and one of the quickest set of legs in the County, entered Morristown high school. "I started high school with a dream in my mind," says Marvin. "My dream was to have success in the classroom and on the basketball court. I hoped to have enough success that some small college might pay my way to have me come play for them." Not only did Wood dream about having such success—he worked hard to make his dream come true.

Indiana high school basketball was different in 1942 than it is today. Players were generally shorter and did not shoot as well or as often as modern players. The rules provided one freethrow for every non-shooting foul and each quarter began with a "jump ball." Offensive and defensive strategies were focused more towards team play than towards exploiting the talents of one or two exceptional players. Scores were generally lower and even incidental contact was considered a foul.

Before consolidation swallowed up hundreds of small community high schools, small towns through out the state had their own high school. Some were quite small, and, while many could not field football or baseball teams, all had basketball programs. Nearly every county had five or six schools with enrollments of less than two hundred students. The communities supporting these small schools displayed a fierce pride in their basketball teams.

In a time before television and shopping malls, Friday or Saturday night basketball games brought out the businessmen, homemakers, laborers, and students. Games were often played in cramped gymnasiums with less than two feet between the baselines and the bleachers or walls. Sometimes five or six hundred fans would cram themselves into facilities with only enough seats for four hundred. The games provided a common interest for the community and an excellent place to socialize while rooting for the home team.

In the forties over eight hundred high school teams competed for the state championship. The large number of high schools throughout the state gave hundreds of young men an opportunity to play ball. High school basketball players were celebrities, enjoying the adoration or enduring the scorn of the entire community. The pressure on coaches, too, was tremendous. It seemed that every Tom, Dick, and Mary knew what was best for their community's basketball team.

The community of Morristown was not unlike other communities in this respect. Unfortunately, they'd gone for some time without so much as a county championship. With their frustration several coaches had come and gone. Then a hard-working coach, Gerl Furr, and a dynamic little guard, Marvin Wood, changed all of that.

In Marvin's first season at Morristown which boasted a student population of one hundred fifty, Marvin blossomed into an excellent player. His willingness to work hard and his quick, heady play impressed his new coach and the town. In his freshman season Marvin helped lead Morristown to the school's first sectional championship.

The Yellow Jackets were not expected to be good in '42. A dearth of talented upper-classmen made their chances for a successful season unlikely. Even so, coach Furr conditioned, coached, and cajoled his team. Preaching team play and hard work, he had them "hitting on all cylinders" by the season's end.

In the sectional tournament the Yellow Jackets upset Fairland and then went on to sting Shelbyville, a much larger school, for the championship. As a freshman guard on an that inexperienced team, Marvin accomplished a rare feat by being named to the all-sectional team. His season, however, did not start out that way.

"We worked hard for coach Furr—harder than I'd ever worked in sports. After a few of his practices I developed a blister on the ball of my foot," Wood recalls. "Then on my way home from school one day I stepped on a walnut and bruised the blister. It soon became infected and I had to miss about six weeks of basketball. My abscence put me behind the others and I was worried about being able to play.

"We were a little shy of talent in the upper classes and I was mature for my age. So when I healed I got an opportunity to start on the varsity . . . We weren't good that year. I think we ended the season at 7-10." Wood saw team play as the key that turned things around during the sectional. "When I started working out with the starting unit, they could have given me a hard time since I was a freshman, but they didn't. In fact, they tried to help me. Charlie Rouse, one of our seniors, was one such guy. A hard-nosed competitor, he played aggressive defense and led us by setting a good example. I give him credit for helping me become a good defensive player. As I look back at that team, I can honestly say I don't know how we managed to win the sectional. We were not flashy at all, just a steady bunch of farm boys who played well together."

Morristown played cross-County rival Fairland in the sectional semi-final. The game was a nip and tuck affair. Neither team could muster anything more than a two point spread. Tied 11-11 at the end of the first half, the Yellow Jackets buzzed through to a 17-13 lead with four minutes left in the third quarter. Morristown nursed that lead into the later stages of the fourth quarter when Coach Furr used Marvin's ballhandling ability to drain the clock. Morristown went on to a 32-30 victory over the county champs.

In the championship game against Shelbyville, held in the Bears gym, Morristown pulled off what the local papers referred to as "the upset of the year." Shelbyville had beaten highly-regarded Columbus in their afternoon game and their fans were already discussing a probable regional match-up against down-state powerhouse Madison. But that scenario was not to be as the Yellow Jackets fashioned an upset. The early minutes of the game found both teams sluggish. Marvin got the game's first two points nearly four minutes into the first quarter. The teams then traded baskets until a Bear freethrow cut the Morristown margin to one point, but as the quarter came to an end Marvin hit a long shot to put the Yellow Jackets up 8-5.

A patient offense and a suffocating defense helped Morristown to a 13-9 halftime lead. During the intermission fans from around the county could be heard talking about the steady play of the freshman, Marvin Wood. Wood and his teammates had the folks from Shelbyville plenty worried.

In the third quarter, however, the Bears came out of hibernation and quickly erased the Morristown lead. With the score tied at 13 and the partisan crowd breathing a little easier, Marvin hit a jump shot and put the Yellow Jackets back in front. He then stole a pass and added two more points to his tally. Shelbyville responded with a basket and a freethrow to close the gap to one point at the end of three quarters.

Near the start of the fourth quarter Marvin began to suffer from leg cramps and had to leave the game. During his absence Shelbyville took their first lead of the game 20-18. With his team down, Marvin reentered the game and immediately fed his teammate, Charlie Rouse, under the basket which led to a bucket and a tie game. After a Shelbyville freethrow, the Yellow

Jackets came back with another bucket. Finally, tied 22-22 with less than two minutes remaining, Morristown held the ball for one last shot. With twenty-two seconds to play Fred John drove to the hoop and hit a layup. Shelbyville was unable to score on their next possession and the Morristown Yellow Jackets were left to celebrate their first-ever sectional championship.

"In the Shelbyville game we won by holding the ball. It was a gutsy bit of strategy from our coach, but it was the right call." As Wood recounts the strategy employed by Furr, a wry grin comes to his face. "I give Gerl Furr credit for helping me to understand tempo. He taught me early in my career how effective a change-of-pace or slow-down game can be. He was probably the single most important factor for our success."

Regarding his selection to the All-Sectional team, Wood modestly explains: "I think they picked me because they felt they had to have someone from the winning team on the all-sectional roster." Even so, Furr and several of Marv's teammates thought he deserved the honor. "Marvin was one of the better players I coached," says Furr. "I'll tell you this: I don't know if he was good enough to be all-sectional or whatever, but there is no way we could have won without him."

Marvin's good friend and teammate, Harold McWilliams agrees, "When Marvin was in the game I always felt we had a chance to win. He had a knack for doing the right things out there and I enjoyed the chance to play with a guy like Marvin. In that sectional championship, every time it looked like Shelbyville was going to do us in, up stepped Marvin to hit a bucket, or make a steal, or get an assist. We wouldn't have won without him and we were plenty worried when he pulled up hurt in the fourth quarter."

During the next three years Morristown continued to be a basketball force. In three of Marvin's four seasons, Morristown lost fewer than five games; won the tough Shelby County tournament twice; and gave the larger schools an especially tough time. The Yellow Jackets played good basketball and always in front of a packed gym.

An interesting aspect of Marvin's high school basketball years is that he played ball with two of his brothers. Wayne joined the team when Marvin was a sophomore and John played when Marvin was a senior. All were good ballplayers and quickly insist that the others were the better. For example, Marvin and John both agree that Wayne was the better defensive player while Wayne and Marvin say that John was the better offensive player. Regarding Marvin both brothers grin and kiddingly admit that he's been darn lucky.

Marvin and his brothers shared an enthusiasm for basketball typical of Hoosier boys. They weren't very tall, but refused to let a lack of height stop them from competing. They found ways to compensate for their short statures. John, who later attended Indiana University where he played for Branch Mc Cracken's "Hurrin' Hoosiers," went to coach Furr to see if there was some way he could improve his jumping ability. He figured that he'd never be able to dunk the ball, but maybe with a little work he could touch the rim. Furr got him a length of rope which they hung from the rafters in the barn. Every day John would go out and jump up to touch the rope. When he was able to touch it they would raise the rope an inch and he'd continue to work at jumping up and touching it. This went on until he was able to touch the end of a rope ten feet above the the barn floor.

Marvin, on the other hand, had a different method of negating the effectiveness of taller opponents. He'd place himself between his man and the basket and then by using his quickness he'd "screen" his opponent until the ball was within his reach. On offense he'd simply fake and then "turn on the gas" towards the hoop. Marvin's "deceptive speed" is often noted in newspaper reports of his high school and college games.

Wayne, the biggest of the Wood boys, achieved his objectives on the court through the use of brute strength. He played in the middle and although many of his opponents were taller they always dreaded having to contend with Wayne's somewhat unorthodox style of play. In one game Wayne was having trouble guarding a center from neighboring Fairland. This fellow would "hook" Wayne with his left elbow, knocking him out of the way to clear a path to the basket. Coach Furr instructed him to close that lane to the basket, and when Wayne complained about his opponents illegal tactics, Coach Furr reminded him that he was big enough to take care of himself and to cut off that lane to the basket or he'd find somebody else who could.

Wayne went back out on the court and did as he was told. Every time his opponent threw up his elbow to hook Wayne, Wayne would reach down and pull the hair on the fellow's leg. This went on for the better part of the second half and by the

1943 Morristown Sectional Champions: Front row left to right: Bob Ross, Mascot Bruce Furr, Tommie Lee. Row 2: Jim Adams, Charlie Rouse, Dwight Wortman, Fred John, Marvin Wood. Row 3: Manager Harold Smith, Berl Miller, Carl Hawkins, Harold McWilliams, Coach Gerl Furr.

time the game was over the opposing center was ready for a fist fight. Wayne had to be escorted from the gym under the protection of his coach and teammates—But he did shut down the middle.

The Wood boys were excellent basketball players, but their athletic talents did not end there. The boys also played softball. Small schools like Morristown did not have the means to field baseball teams, so they fielded softball teams. Marvin pitched and played shortstop, Wayne caught and played first base, and John played in the infield or outfield. Every year Gerl Furr, who coached all of the sports programs at Morristown, entered the High School's softball team in the Shelbyville Men's Summer League. The high school team, which employed a daring approach to the game, not unlike that of St. Louis Cardinal's "Gas House Gang," played in front of large crowds that showed up to watch the high school boys tangle with the Fraternal Order of Police, the local bank employees, and so forth.

On one memorable night the boys played until well past midnight. Both Marvin and his opponent pitched twelve innings of shut-out softball. The game had to be called on account of the late hour. To this day Furr insists that Marvin's last strikeout was accomplished without the ball ever leaving his hand. The grin on Wayne's face when asked by Furr about that last out would seem to indicate that Wayne had a knack for slapping his hand in a catcher's mitt making it sound like a softball.

In Marvin's junior season the fruits of coach Furr's labors began to blossom. "In my junior year we were tough," recalls Marvin. "We beat everybody in everything. In basketball we won the county tournament, but we did not win the sectional. In fact, our sectional loss was only our second defeat. We lost both games to Hope. They had Bill Shepherd, one of the better players of the day. Years later he and I were teammates at Butler. Bill led Hope to the sweet sixteen that year. They beat us during the regular season and then again in the finals of the sectional."

During his junior year Marvin suffered a broken collarbone which kept him off the court for over four weeks. His time away reduced his ability to help his team during the sectional. "We were playing Fairland and somebody came by before the game and said 'We're gonna get you,'" Marvin recalls. "That happened every now and then, players would make comments like that. On this night, however, somebody did undercut me while I was trying to make a break-away layup. I landed on my head which knocked me out and when I woke up I discovered that I'd broken my collarbone. The injury came at a bad time because we were only four weeks from the sectional and the fracture would take about four to six weeks to heal.

"In the sectional I played in the afternoon game against Columbus. We won but I reinjured myself. In the championship game against Hope I played but was not much help. We lost. We'd been ranked in the top twenty that year which made the injury and Sectional loss even more frustrating because we thought we had a good chance to go a long way."

While sports dominated Marvin's high school days, his four years at Morristown High prepared him for life after high school too. Realizing that college would require hours of studying, Marvin developed good study habits. With plenty of chores at home and little free time, he made it a point to complete all of his studies while he was at school. "I learned to treat school like another job," says Marvin. "When the work was done, I could take it easy." He confesses that school did not come easy for him and he had to work hard to maintain a "B" average.

Marvin, a popular student with many friends, admits that he was a shy high school student. Girls found him attractive and some even pestered him for dates. Marvin, on the other hand, was uninterested in girls. He felt uncomfortable around them. In fact, he managed to avoid dating until his good friend Harold McWilliams talked him into going out. "One day Harold came up to me in study hall, I think he owed me a favor or something, anyway he asked me if I had a choice of girls to go out with who would I choose," Marvin recalls with a laugh. "I told him I wanted a date with Shirley Tracy because she wouldn't go out with any of the older guys. Harold asked her if she would go out with me and she said yes. I can still remember sitting in study hall when she came up to tell me that she would go out with me. My voice squeaked and I could hardly talk to that girl.

"I remember when I went to her house on the night of the date. There must have been five or six cars of older guys sitting down the block from her home—they followed us every place we went. It was a dull, boring evening because I felt like I had ten or twelve guys in the backseat."

By the time he was a junior, Marvin had developed a definite plan for dating. "I remember someone in my family advising me to be careful when chosing whom to go out with—because you never know who you are going to fall in love with," he relates. "Remembering those words, I decided I ought to have a list of qualities as to what I'd like in a potential mate. I probably started that list late in my sophomore year.

"I looked at my mother as a role model when it came to thinking about someone I might marry. I tried to think of the things that she did to make our home so happy. My mother was a good Christian woman and a hard worker so I thought it very important that my wife be a hard-working Christian too. I appreciated the way my mother kept things in order. I didn't like to see beds left unmade or clothes strewn all around. I had brothers who were messy and while I don't consider myself to be picky about such things, I wanted to live in a home that was well managed.

"I wanted a mate who would bring out the best in me, and I hoped to do the same for her. As a backward, shy person, I wanted someone who'd stand up for me, who'd push me to be the best I could be. I wanted a wife who could meet and get along with other people. People were an important part of my life. Of course, any potential mate would have to enjoy sports too because I hoped to be involved in coaching."

Mary Lou, Marvin's wife for over forty years, laughs as Marvin ticks off his list of priorities. It just so happened that the young lady who possessed all of those characteristics was a classmate of his and had been looking at him under criteria of her own. Mary Lou recalls thinking of Marvin this way: "Oh, he was good. He just was 'Mr. Goody two-shoes.' He didn't do anything to get in trouble. I thought he was real nice, he was friendly to me and I to him, but I didn't really think much about him beyond that. I knew he had girls chasing him. The fact that he wasn't interested in them impressed me. Marvin was a serious person. He was involved in sports and he didn't cut-up a lot. He was always a cut above the rest."

It took Marvin a long time to ask Mary Lou for a date. "That happened during the last month of our senior year," he recalls. "We were both at an athletic banquet, but not as a couple. That night I asked her if I could take her home. We'd been classmates and friends for four years. I don't know when it started, but I began to see many of the same qualities in her that I'd put on my list. I knew that she was a Christian. I knew that she was a good worker. She was a good student and we had a lot in common.

"One thing that stands out in my mind about Mary Lou is that she always stood up for what she thought was right. I remember one time in our government class when the teacher changed some grades for athletes. Mary Lou was not an athlete and thus did not get her grade changed. She complained that this was not fair, and while I don't think she got the grade changed, she impressed me by standing up for something that she thought was right.

"I remember another occasion when we voted on the attire for our graduation ceremony. We had more guys in the senior class than girls and all of the guys voted for caps and gowns while all of the girls voted for formals. The girls were upset with the outcome and some were refusing to vote on the color of the caps and gowns. Mary Lou was a good sport and reminded the gals that by voting they could at least get the color they wanted."

On the night Marvin asked Mary Lou to let him give her a ride home she quickly agreed. "After watching my classmates chase him for four years, I decided I might like to date him myself," says Mary Lou. "I let my fourteen-year-old sister, Vera Lee, drive our family car home while Marvin and I followed her. I was frightened that something might happen to her and I was excited to be with Marvin."

Aside from his blossoming romance, other important decisions loomed on the horizon for Marvin. Throughout his high school years the tragedies and triumphs of World War II were much on the mind of his community. Two of Marvin's former teammates, Charlie Rouse and Dwight Wortman, had been killed in the conflict (Marvin and Harold McWilliams were the first recipients of the Rouse-Wortman Memorial Award which was given to outstanding young athletes at Morristown high school.). Marvin and his classmates often wondered what might happen to them when they became elgible for the draft.

Marvin Wood (left) and Harold McWilliams winners of the first Rouse-Wortman Award. Presented in 1946 by Laurence Wortman in memory of Marvin's classmates Dwight Wortman and Charlie Rouse who were killed in WWII.

Shortly after his eighteenth birthday, Marvin's draft board called him in for a physical. While Marvin waited to hear of his fate, several of his friends decided that they'd rather enlist in the Navy than be drafted by the Army. They wanted Marvin to join them, but he explained that he was a lousy swimmer and would wait to hear from his draft board. Six months later the draft board, encouraged by the surrender of Germany, began to provide exemptions for college-bound high school seniors. Thus Marvin Wood was one of the lucky ones who was not asked to bear arms in defense of his country.

Marvin's high school graduation picture 1946.

By the end of his senior year, Marvin's basketball prowess earned him a spot as one of the state's top one hundred athletes. Even so, he had yet to receive any scholarship offers. Disappointed but undaunted he made plans to enroll in Ball State during the Fall with the objective of getting a degree in education. Those plans changed, however, when friends in the community made his case before Butler University's basketball coach, Tony Hinkle. Herb Schwomeyer, Freshman coach at Butler, had officiated several of Marvin's games and thought Marvin might be able to help out at Butler. Robert Hurst, a Butler alumnus, drove Marvin to Indianapolis to meet Coach Hinkle. Hinkle was impressed and three weeks before the Fall semester he offered Marvin a scholarship to play basketball at Butler University. Marvin gladly accepted.

In a period of eight months Marvin's fate had been twice changed. He would not be going to war nor would he attend college as a student only. Ahead of him lay four tuition-free years at Butler University under the guidance of one of the brightest minds in basketball. Some would call it luck. Marvin saw it as a positive answer to his prayers and hard work.

*Returning Varsity players 1947-48 from left to right: Ralph "Buckshot"
O'Brien, Bob Evans, Charlie Maas, John Barrowcliff, Bill Shepherd,
Jimmy Doyle and Marvin Wood.*

3

Butler University
1946-1950

In the months after VE day, thousands of US servicemen came home from war to begin again their lives. Many of these servicemen, encouraged by the government's promise to provide them with an education, headed off to college, swamping the nation's universities which struggled to handle this sudden swelling of the student population.

Butler University was not unlike other institutions in this respect. The student population, which normally ranged from between 2500-3500 students, swelled to over 5000 for the 1946 Fall semester. While colleges such as Butler had previously been utilized by young men and women in their late teens and early twenties, many of the returning servicemen were older. Their experiences in war gave them a different perspective than that which had previously prevailed within the "ivy towers." This influx of older, less frivolous students, brought a different attitude about accepted behavior on campus. Time honored traditions such as freshmen wearing "rhinie pots," or a "seniors only" sidewalk were cast aside in favor of more practical behavior.

Marvin Wood started his college years in this environment. "When I began college and saw all of the servicemen back from World War II, I knew the future was going to be a competitive one," recalls Marvin. "I could sense a high level of intelligence and maturity in the returning veterans. I knew that eventually I'd be competing with them for job opportunities. Knowing this I began to understand that I'd better get prepared or life was not going to be easy."

Marvin found college classwork much more demanding than his high school studies. English and history were two courses that especially gave him trouble. "I've always felt that I'd gotten a good education in English, but when I got to college—boy-oh-boy did I struggle . . . In history I liked the course, but we had reading assignments and many times they would include over one hundred pages of reading. I'd never had to read so much in such a short period of time—and my professor not only expected us to read the material, but to be able to discuss it as well."

The study habits Marvin acquired in high school served him well in college. He treated school like a job and spent nine to ten hours a day dividing his time between course work and basketball. In addition to his studies and basketball, Marv's scholarship required him to work. He and two other student athletes had the responsibility of lining the football fields three times each week.

One of the biggest challenges Marvin faced in his first year was making the basketball team. "When we first discussed my going to Butler, I thought my chances of making the team were slim," he recalls. "Butler played a big-time schedule. They played all of the Big Ten schools except Minnesota and Iowa. Butler was also a member of the Mid-America Conference which many sportswriters thought was one of the toughest basketball conferences in the country. Our schedule included tough independent schools like Notre Dame. Coach Hinkle had a successful basketball program and for me to have a chance to become a member of it was a dream come true.

"Tryouts in my freshman year were a nightmare. Over two hundred guys tried out. Many were returning veterans, some had lettered years before or during the war. I competed against guys who were in their middle or late twenties. We had fights every day in practice. I don't think Uncle Sam did much to help some of those guys with their basketball, but he sure taught them how to fight. I made the team that year, but primarily because I was on scholarship."

Marvin's college career began with him on the bench of the junior varsity squad. Behind two returning servicemen on the depth chart, he did not expect he'd play much—and then fate again stepped in and changed his fortunes. "We were set to play a JV game at 6:00 one night and two of the guys who started before me did not show up on time—they thought the game started at 6:30. I started that game and played well. In fact, I played well enough to be moved in front of those guys in the depth chart.

"A week or so later, Coach Hinkle, whose varsity squad was struggling, had us scrimmage his third-string varsity team. We beat them. He had us come back the next day and scrimmage his first string. We were beating them after about thirty minutes of play. As a result of those scrimmage sessions, Hinkle demoted some of his varsity players and promoted Jim Rosenstihl, Gerald McCarty, Gene O'Neil, and me to the varsity squad."

As a freshman on the varsity team, Marvin saw little playing time. "If I got in the game we were either way ahead or way behind, but I didn't care. I tried to pay attention to what was going on. By doing so I learned a lot. I think sitting on the bench helped to give me a unique perspective which has helped me in my career as a coach. I can sympathize with players who ride the pine and I also understand what the guys on the floor are going through."

Marvin adds that just being a part of the team was a thrill. "Coach Hinkle made being a member of his basketball team exciting," recalls Marvin. "He was a man ahead of his time. Hinkle coached a smaller college that played a big-time schedule. Imagine a school of twenty-five hundred students playing a basketball schedule with I.U., Purdue, Notre Dame, Michigan, and so on. Yet, we played 'em tough. Coach Hinkle was the main reason we were able to do that.

"He had the ability to take small-town players and turn then into a good team. He was able to do this because of his 'Hinkle System.' 'The Hinkle' is a continuity approach to basketball. He'd broken the game down into one man, two man, or three man drills and then combined them together into a five man unit. The goal of the system is to have two people playing with the ball at the same time. Two people would play with the ball and the other three guys would have the responsibility to keep the defense entertained by setting picks or making cuts away from the ball."

"...a lot of the guys who played for Coach Hinkle ended up in the coaching profession. Guys like Bob Evans, Marvin Cave, Jim Rosenstihl, Charlie Maas, Walt Fields, Bill Shepherd, Jimmy Doyle, we all had ambitions of becoming high school coaches. We made it and I believe that any success we've enjoyed came as a result of Hinkle's continuity offense and the two and three man drills he used to teach it. By giving us such tools Hink gave us a headstart on most other young coaches."

The Hinkle system, sometimes called the "Butler Offense," involves basic basketball drills such as pass-and-cut and pick-and-roll. The continuity system offers versatility to adjust according to the type of personnel. Hinkle was a student of the games he coached. He learned about attacking defenses and defending against offenses from football which, at the time Marvin played at Butler, was far ahead of basketball in the area of strategy. Hinkle applied football knowledge to the game of basketball and came up with a complete system built on fundamentals.

Bill Shepherd who played three seasons for Hinkle at Butler and went on to coach recalls seeing the "Hinkle System" for the

"Butler" Offense:

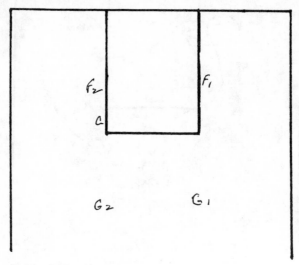

Fig. 1. Butler Alignment
   Note: Center could play high or low post.

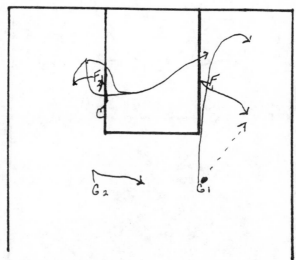

Fig. 2. G1 initiates the offense by passing to F1 and
   then cutting. Meanwhile C picks for F1 who
   cuts through the center.

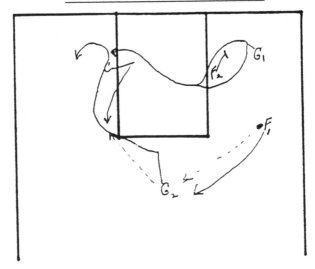

Fig. 3. F1 passes to G2 and follows the ball. G1 passes to C and cuts while G2 picks G1's man.

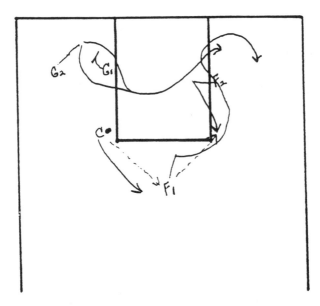

Fig. 4. Continuity continues with each player.

first time. "I played for I.U. my first year of college and I didn't get to play much. On the bench during our game against Butler, I noticed them picking, rolling, passing, cutting and all of the sudden the ball would be in the basket. I'd never seen anything like it before. Each guy had something to do and the whole team seemed to move like clock work. They did not have near the talent that we did, yet, they were in the game and it took a superb effort from our leading scorer for us to beat them."

In addition to being an innovator, Coach Hinkle understood the notion of team play. He did not always use the best individual players, but rather, he tried to find seven or eight guys who worked well together. Such an approach to the game enabled a team player like Marvin to fit right in. Perhaps, under different circumstances, Marvin may have become a starting player at Butler, or even a star. The basketball team, however, had been blessed with a pair of bookend guards from the Indianapolis area, Jimmy Doyle and Ralph (Buckshot) O'Brien. O'Brien and Doyle were one of the best guard tandems in the country, and perhaps two of the best players to ever play at Butler. Both were tremendous shooters and excellent playmakers. In describing his college career Marvin laughingly admits: "I never did become an All American, but I guarded one in practice for four years."

During his time at Butler Marvin developed life-long friendships with many of his teammates. "We had a unique chemistry on that team," he recalls. "Bill, Jim, and I were from small towns. Guys like Buckshot and Doyle they were from the big city but kind of green. We played with older guys—John Barrowcliff, Charlie Maas, Marvin Cave, and Herod Toon. Some of those guys had been to war and had seen the world. We had a lot of different perspectives and I think we all had a tremendous amount of respect for each other. We learned a lot by being teammates. Of course, basketball back then was not the serious business that it is today. Sure, we loved to compete and played our hardest, but when we were out there together we always had a lot of fun too."

Marvin Cave, who coached for several years at Frankfort and later became an executive with Eli Lilly, recalls his playing days with Marvin. "Some of us were returning veterans and we'd seen an awful lot, then there were fellas like Woody, who were little more than country boys. We got a kick out of watching them develop. We used to rib them something awful, especially

Woody." During Marvin's freshman season Butler's starting five included Big "Jawn" Barrowcliff, Herod Toon, Charlie Maas, Jimmy Doyle, and Ralph "Buckshot" O'Brien. Bill Shepherd, Bob Evans, and Jerry Cranny played important roles while Cave, Walt Fields, Jim Rosenstihl, and Marvin all saw limited action.

Being short and nearly bald, "Woody," as his buddies called him, was the butt of many locker room pranks. The incident most often recalled by his teammates involves an empty Vatalis hair tonic bottle and a fake urinalysis test. Without going into much detail, let's just say the test was a difficult one. Marvin took these good-natured pranks in the spirit in which they were intended and was known to have perpetrated a few himself.

In Marvin's freshman year the Bulldogs were 14-7 and the junior varsity squad lost only one game. The varsity had lost several games late in the season which cost them the Indiana College Conference championship. They did share the Mid-American title with Cincinnati and they whipped a good I.U. ballclub. The superb effort from the JV squad, coupled with the fact that Butler would not lose a single varsity starter to graduation, gave Bulldog fans hope that their basketball team would be tough for years to come.

While he'd enjoyed some success on the basketball court, Marvin's first year grade-point average left him concerned about his future. His academic performance had fallen well short of what he'd hoped. Despite his excellent study habits, he had trouble making the adjustment from high school to college. One of the biggest problems he faced was learning how to use the library. Coming from a small town he had never seen a library as large as the one at Butler and learning how to use it was a challenge.

His struggle with academics has given him a understanding of what it is like for student athletes to cope with the dual demands of athletics and scholarship. He believes hard work and perserverance, invaluable tools on the basketball court, are also the tools with which to meet such challenges.

"I can't imagine that it is any tougher today than it was back then, but I think I may have had some advantages over young people today—I lived through a depression and saw how hard folks had to struggle to survive. Young people today don't have experiences like that. The world is much different now. Thank goodness times are easier, but nowadays kids struggling with course work as I did might just give up because they figure that life is not supposed to be so hard. As I look back, I cherish every good grade I got. I earned every one of them. I'm proud of my college degree because I worked hard to get it."

His grades being much lower than he'd hoped they'd be, Marvin thought about quitting college during the summer after his freshman year. He spent the summer working with his uncle Harold on the milk route and gave serious consideration to quitting college to find work elsewhere. Marvin discussed these things with his mother, who knew how much he'd always wanted to be a coach and educator. She talked him into spending at least one more year at Butler. When Marvin headed back to school for his second year he told his mother that he was doing it for her. She was not impressed. "Marvin," she said, "that simply will not work. If you're to be successful in school, you're going to have to do it for yourself—not for me." Armed with his mother's admonishment, Marvin headed back for Indianapolis.

* *

Butler University left a positive impression on Marvin Wood. He is grateful for the dedication of his professors and is quick to point out that his mentors at Butler were not only intelligent, but also friendly and quite helpful. Mary Elizabeth Smith, his English instructor, is one he fondly recalls. "Professor Smith could explain English in a way that was meaningful to me," he recalls. "She was a wonderful person and one of the best teachers I've ever had. I'd been in English classes where I felt like I was way out in left field, but Professor Smith's class was different. She made learning fun.

"Beyond her abilities as an English instructor, she was a good person. I think she sort of adopted my class. Once I asked to be excused for a baseball game and half-way through it I looked up in the stands and there she sat with all of my classmates. On another occasion she had us attend a musical performance where a classmate was performing. She treated us like family and that made us want to do our best. She made a positive impression on me."

Professors like Ms. Smith did much to help Marvin get through school. His years at Butler gave him an education both in and out of the classroom. "Those were four of the greatest learning years in my life," he explains. "Once I got away from home and the small town environment, I discovered that people see things differently. I had to evaluate and make decisions as to what I would tolerate, or how I would accept certain things that I did not necessarily agree with. I use alcohol and cigarettes as one example. As an athlete and a Christian, these were things that did not interest me. I knew alcohol and tobacco were not good, yet, some very good people were using them.

"I never took an interest in alcohol or tobacco, but I have some great friends who did. I don't know of one of them who let it effect their performance on the basketball court, in the classroom, or in their personal lives. They behaved responsibly. If I learned anything at all in college, I learned not to judge folks by their little habits, but rather, by their lives as a whole. I learned to make the compromises necessary to maintain healthy relationships with people whose views might not coincide with my own."

* *

The Bulldogs had a fine season during Marvin's sophomore year. Their 16-7 record included victories against Purdue and Indiana. Doyle, O'Brien, and Maas blossomed into All-Americans and the entire squad seemed to improve with each game. Marvin saw little action that year, but when he did play he performed well. His skills as a defender and ballhandler worried opponents. Late in one game against Purdue, Coach Hinkle gave Marvin the ball and had him dribble circles around Boilermaker defenders who looked like boys chasing a frisky dog who'd stolen their ball. In another game against Ohio State, a Buckeye fan, frustrated with Marvin's quickness and agility, was heard yelling "Step on him!"

1949-50 returning varsity players from right to left. Back row: Marvin Wood, Gene Stohler and Buckshot O'Brien. Front row: Jimmy Doyle, Ralph Chapman, Dee Baker and Coach Paul "Tony" Hinkle.

Marvin never became too frustrated with the fact that he did not get to play as much as he would have liked. He sees the time he spent on the bench as a benefit. He always tried to get a seat next to the coach to find out what he was thinking or noticing out on the court. This approach helped him to be prepared to enter the game.

In the classroom Marvin's positive attitude and experience from the previous year began to make a difference. "I found in my sophomore year that I covered twice as much ground with each step I took. As a freshman I worried about the papers I had to turn in. I simply did not know where to go to get the information I needed to complete the paper. As a sophomore I knew where to go to get information. I was beginning to learn how to put that information together in a more clear and concise fashion. I just felt a lot more comfortable. I felt like a college student, where, when I was a freshman, I felt like a high school student floundering my way through this huge institution."

During Marvin's second year he commuted from his parents farm in Morristown, rising early to drive a '39 chevy into Indianapolis. He'd return late in the evening after a day of school, work, and practice. When time allowed Marvin continued to court Mary Lou Henley. Early in his sophomore year he decided she was the woman with whom he'd like to share his life. On his mother's birthday, 03 October 1947, he asked for her hand in marriage. She accepted and they set a wedding date of 03 September 1948.

Mary Lou is absolutely radiant as she remembers that time in their lives. "When I first graduated from high school I had planned to go to Ball State, but then my mother and I had a discussion about college and she said there'd be more money for some of the extras if I stayed at home and worked for a year. I thought it was a good idea so I kept my job at the Bluebird in Morristown and found work in Indianapolis at the Chevrolet plant.

"Later, my sister Rita and I moved to Indianapolis and, all along, Marvin and I dated on the weekends."

After Marvin's freshman year Mary Lou and her parents again discussed college. "At that time I told them that Marvin and I were getting serious and he might ask me to marry him. We agreed then that I would work and not go to school. Even so, I wasn't sure I wanted to be engaged for the three years it would take him to finish school. A month later he asked me to marry him and, three more years or not, I wasn't about to turn him down.

"Marvin gave me a ring in October and we set the wedding date for September of the next year. The months that followed were some of the happiest and busiest of my life. We had a large living room in our house and I remember on the Fourth of July my mother had satin from one end of the room to the other. She made my wedding dress and the bridesmaids dresses too. My sister Rita Mae was my maid of honor. My sister Vera Lee and a friend from work, Mona Hopkins were bridesmaids. Marvin's brother, Wayne, was the best man. His brothers John and Keith were ushers.

Wedding photo 03 September 1948.

"The wedding was a joyous event. Marvin was beaming and many of our friends came to celebrate with us. The church, adorned with honeysuckle vines and dimly lit with candles, was beautiful. I'll never forget the scent of the honeysuckle. I guess about the only bad thing that happened occurred when I came to the church to dress. I saw some of my cousins from Ohio and I hadn't seen them for quite some time. Anyway, I went over and hugged them and said hello, but when I got downstairs to dress I found that the ring bearer's pillow I'd been carrying did not have Marvin's wedding ring on it. My mother and I just about died. I figured that it had to be up in the yard where I'd greeted my cousins and, sure enough, we found it lying there in the grass."

The newlyweds left for Cincinnati that night behind the wheel of Marvin's dad's new Chrysler.

"We were in Cincinnati for our honeymoon and had planned tocatch a ballgame, visit museums, and so forth," Mary Lou recalls. "On Saturday we saw the Reds play the Cardinals and when we got back to the hotel Marvin mentioned something about his semi-pro baseball team, wondering how they would do in their game which was to be played back in Indianapolis the next day. Well, this is where I made my first mistake. I told him we could go back if he really wanted to. Sure enough, on Sunday morning he was packed and ready to head back home. I suppose he's been spoiled ever since." Back home in Morristown, the Woods took residence in an upstairs apartment where they lived for the next two years.

The question of whether Marvin should go back to college came up again after his sophomore year. This time it had nothing to do with classwork or the basketball team. During the Summer between his sophomore and junior years Marvin landed a job at the International Harvester plant on the East side of Indianapolis working in the gears department. When the summer was nearly over the company announced they were going to expand the gears department and asked Marvin if he could stay on as an inspector. "The salary and benefits they offered were quite tempting," he recalls. "They were prepared to pay me five-fifty an hour, which was half again what a teacher would make. I made more money that summer than I'd made in my entire life. In the end, however, Mary Lou and I both agreed that my dream was to be a coach and educator and that no amount of money would be able to replace that."

So, Marvin went back to college while Mary Lou continued to work at the Chevrolet plant in Indianapolis. They worked odd jobs on the weekends and made the daily commute to Indy with several others who helped pay for the gas and upkeep on the car. Marvin further supplemented their income by hauling eggs to campus which he sold to his coaches and other members of the faculty. Though the change in martial status brought some difficult times financially, both Marvin and Mary Lou describe those first years of marriage as some of happiest days of their lives.

"We'd made a major adjustment in our lives and handled it well—which is not to say that everything went just the way we wanted it to go. Mary Lou and I were blessed with great patience. We did not have everything we wanted, but we didn't have to have everything right then. We knew that better days were ahead of us and that the sacrifices we were making would bear fruit in later years. We had fun while looking forward to those better' days.

"An older couple living in the apartment below us helped us quite a bit. We had a great relationship with them. We shared some evenings and they enlightened us with that wisdom older people have and I think some of the energy younger couples have rubbed off on them . . . We might have been a couple of poor old country kids, but it was a great time in our lives."

The late 1940s were a special time in the history of the United States. Americans, on account of geography and good fortune, were spared the terrible devastation caused by bombs landing on their homes, factories, churches, office buildings, power plants, streets, and so on. Returning servicemen found themselves in the midst of an expanding economy with plenty of room for growth. The factories that once produced the products of war now turned their attention to the wants and needs of material-starved consumers. The nation had emerged from the gloom of a depression and the doom of a war looking for "happy days again."

The cold war lay several years down the road and the nagging questions posed by those who feared the possible effects of nuclear weapons were distant and obscure. Americans wanted nothing more than to pile into their new automobiles and head to the beach or ballpark for a weekend's worth of good, old-fashioned fun. They worked hard and they played hard.

The attraction of sports was never higher and games of all kinds were well-attended. During the Winter, basketball became the sport of choice and Americans came to the college games en masse. At Butler University, for example, the fieldhouse, which seated 14,000, was packed for almost every game.

The popularity of the sport brought with it the attraction of gambling on the outcome of games. When Marvin played at Butler, the Bulldog games were always handicapped by book-makers and plenty of money passed hands as a result of their victories or defeats. When Marvin was a sophomore, a certain party in Brooklyn tried to get a teammate to "shave points" in a game against Ohio University. Charlie Maas, a starting guard-forward and one of the Bulldogs star players, received a letter in the mail which read:

> "Hello Charley: A friend has seen you play and you sure impressed him.
>
> We are impressed in you. I have a business proposition for you which may be of benefit. I would appreciate having a prompt reply."

Coach Hinkle was suspicious of the letter, but did not want to deny his player any legitimate job offer. He had Maas send a reply simply stating that Charlie would entertain any reasonable offer to play ball after graduation.

On the Friday night before the Ohio U. game which the "bookies" had picked Butler to win by at least nine points, Charlie Maas received a phone call from a Brooklyn man who said that he was interested in seeing Butler win by less than nine points. He added that he was so interested in the game's outcome that he'd give Maas $500.00 to insure the point spread would be less than nine. Charlie got mad, told the caller he wanted no part of it, and then reported the incident to Hinkle who, in turn, notified the authorities.

The caller was never apprehended but he would have lost money if he'd bet on Ohio against that point spread. Maas, "all steamed up about the low value placed on his character," took the first five shots against Ohio and hit three of them. The Bulldogs went on to steamroll the Bobcats 59-34. This incident, coupled with "point shaving" scandals at Brooklyn College and George Washington University, showed Charlie and his teammates how vulnerable college athletes were to the ill-intentions of men using the game to make an illegal profit. "Yes," Marvin recalls shaking his head, "I think that really surprised us. Five-hundred dollars was quite a bit of money back then. We kidded each other about the incident, but it sure made me appreciate the integrity in all of us who played the game."

During Marvin's junior year, the Bulldogs had one of the finest teams in the school's history. Five returning seniors, nine juniors, heighth, good shooters, and excellent ball handlers gave Butler high hopes for the 48-49 season. Unfortunately, a red hot Illinois ball club and a determined Ohio State squad had them limping home after their first two games with an 0-2 record.

From that auspicious beginning the team caught fire and won eleven straight games including triumphs against Indiana and Purdue. They defeated the number-one ranked team in the country, Cincinnati, 74-52 and then travelled to New York to take on Claire Bee's highly-touted Long Island squad. The trip involved a couple of firsts for Marvin. It was the first time he'd ever flown on an airplane and the first time he'd ever been in "The Big Apple."

"For a wide-eyed country boy, New York was simply overwhelming," Marvin recalls. "We saw tall buildings everywhere we went. I got a sore neck from looking up so much. We went to the top of the Empire State Building. Looking down from the top was a little scary. People looked like ants from up there. Coach Hinkle wanted to make that trip a learning experience for us. We saw many of the tourists attractions and ate a nine course dinner at 'Mama Leonia's.' We ate things that night that I'd never heard of.

"We beat Long Island and I remember being surprised at the size of the arena. The floor, however, had a lot of dead, warped spots and played worse than some hay mows I'd played in."

Back home in Indiana the team continued to win until an inspired Notre Dame squad trimmed them 53-52. That loss was especially tough because Butler had a 52-46 lead with less than two minutes remaining. The Bulldogs rebounded from that setback and won their next three games. Unfortunately, their season ended on a down note. They dropped their last two ballgames, one, a rematch against Cincinnati in the Queen City, the other, against lowly Western Reserve which had only won two other ballgames all season. The loss in Cleveland cost the Bulldogs a shot at an NCAA bid (Butler had previously won an NCAA title under Hinkle in 1929, and in 1924 they'd won one under Pat Page when Hinkle was an assistant coach.), but they did share a piece of the Mid-American conference crown with Cincinnati. Their final record of 18-5 was the school's best since 1934.

Although not a member of the starting five, Marvin saw plenty of action during his junior year and became a valuable "sixth man." Hinkle used him in key situations when they needed to get the ball or to hold on to the ball. Marvin made a major contribution to the team that year and hoped to have a chance to become a starter during his senior season.

Marvin uses between the legs pass versus Cincinnati University 1949.

Marvin's performance in the classroom mirrored that of his prowess on the basketball court. He'd overcome many of the difficulties he'd encountered during his first two years. "My junior and senior year just seemed to fly past," he recalls. "School was fun, I was making a contribution to the basketball team, and Mary Lou and I were enjoying our first years together. As my junior year ended it began to occur to me that I would soon be done with school and on to the challenge I'd dreamed of since high school. I would soon become a coach and teacher."

Marvin's senior year proved to be his best year in college. He did well in the classroom and by mid-season he'd become a starting guard. "We'd been having a tough time that year and we were on our way down to Bloomington one night to play Indiana University," he recalls. "They were one of the better teams in the Big Ten. Coach Hinkle took a seat beside me on the bus and said: 'Hey short spokes, I'm going to start you tonight. If we need more size we'll just have to get somebody bigger in there for you.' Well, a young guy loves a challenge and I was determined that he wasn't going to take me out because of my lack of rebounding. We got beat that night, but I played every second of every minute of that game.

"We came back to play Notre Dame a few nights after that and Hinkle told me that I'd get another shot at starting. Notre Dame was a lot bigger than I.U. and I was plenty worried about holding my own on the boards. They also had an all-American guard named Kevin O'Shea and we were not given much of a chance to beat them. I had the best night of my career that night. I led both teams in rebounding; stole the ball from O'Shea four times; and scored eleven points. My teammates and I beat Notre Dame for only the second time in four years."

Notre Dame coach Ed "Moose" Krause provided the by-line for the newspaper reporters that night when he commented: "We were defeated tonight by a little piece of Wood." Marvin had several good games in that stretch. He scored thirteen points against a tough Cincinnati squad and held the ball for several minutes to secure a victory against Ohio University. He and his fellow Bulldogs had a tough year, however, as they ended the season at 12-11. Marvin played in twenty-two of those games, but "Short Spokes" missed the final game of his college career due to a case of the flu.

With the basketball season behind him, Marvin concentrated on his student-teaching which helped prepare him for his teaching career. "I did my student-teaching at Broad Ripple High School under the instruction of Milt Hiatt," he explains. "He taught for a couple of weeks while I observed and then he turned the class over to me. I was a little afraid and nervous about taking over. I'd never taught a class before and I was awed by the number of kids. Broad Ripple was bigger than Morristown and I was still shy about talking to groups of people. Mr. Hiatt helped me get over that and the kids were simply great. I think it helped that I was a college athlete because the kids knew this and thus treated me with a little more respect.

"I taught physical education which had a section in wrestling. Some of the young men wanted to wrestle me because I was smaller. I asked Mr. Hiatt if a teacher should participate in that kind of activity and he assured me that I could handle anything that might come up. I had my doubts because I figured the first ones I'd have to wrestle would be the biggest ones in class. One day while we were working on wrestling the kids badgered me about taking one of them on. Just as I'd figured, they picked the biggest kid in class to tangle with me. As we got down on the mat I was not certain whether this was a wise move or not. Anyway, the bigger, heavier young man took the up position— I had him pinned in about ten seconds. It was just as Mr. Hiatt had told me, I was more mature and thus quicker, stronger and more aggressive. After nailing three of those big kids, a little guy stepped up and said he wanted a try. I'll tell ya, I had my hands full with him!

College graduation photo June 1950.

"The experience at Broad Ripple showed me that kids are generally good-natured and fairly easy to get along with. When the year was over I felt comfortable dealing with the young men and women, but I was still concerned because I did not always know everything that I needed to know. When the time came for me to start interviewing, Coach Hinkle reassured me that I was well-prepared and shouldn't be afraid to tackle any job that was offered. He also told me that nobody knows everything in their first years and that I'd pick up a lot of knowledge along the way. Looking back I must say he was right."

Marvin interviewed with several schools before accepting a position with French Lick, a nice-sized school in the southernmost part of the state. Marvin got the job with help from his friend, Marvin Cave, whose uncle was on the school board.

During the summer after his graduation, Marvin and Mary Lou worked and prepared to move. They purchased a '50 Plymouth and arranged to find a place in their new hometown. The summer passed quickly and, as the approaching fall turned the southern Indiana forests into brightly-colored-flowers of orange and red and purple and yellow, Marvin and Mary Lou headed for French Lick where the beginning of Marvin's career awaited them.

Marvin signs his first contract to coach at French Lick High School. Superintendent J. W. Chambers and Principal J. B. Hammerling look on.

4

French Lick
1950-1952:
A Coaching Debut

French Lick High School circa 1951.

French Lick, a small resort town nestled in the rolling hills of southern Indiana, has a long and storied tradition. Blessed with spring waters purported to have therapeutic value, the town flourished as a retreat for the rich and famous who came to bath and drink "Pluto" water at plush resorts. In the area's heyday, no fewer than eight rail lines ran to the doorsteps of the resorts, bringing hundreds of tourists and pumping thousands of dollars into the local economy.

With the decline of the railroads and advances in medicine, proving the medicinal value of Pluto water to be minimal, the flow of tourists slowed to a trickle and the town fell into a sleepy descent until a youngster named Larry Bird picked up a basketball and put it back on the map.

Marvin Wood came to this hilly resort town in the Fall of 1950 when the trains still brought revelers from Churchill Downs and the foul-tasting "Pluto" water was still being bottled and distributed around the world. Larry Bird had not yet been born, but, as a new head basketball coach with hopes of moving up to a bigger program, Wood would have loved to see Larry's six-foot-nine-inch frame walk down the corridors of the high school.

"One of the most important things any successful coach must have is talent. I was concerned about this when I came to French Lick," Wood confesses. "Coming in I knew that they'd suffered through seven straight losing seasons. I didn't know what type of personnel I'd have, but in looking at the kids in the hallways I knew we weren't going to have much height. French Lick was a nice-sized school with about 350 students. I figured there should be a few good ballplayers in a school of that size. As it turned out we had a couple of kids with a little bit of talent and they were going to be around for a few years."

When Wood held tryouts for his first season he found himself faced with what he describes as the toughest job in coaching. He had to cut several players from the team. "Making cuts has always been extremely difficult for me," he admits. "Usually it boils down to cutting two types of players. Young people who had talent but did not work to improve it, and young people who'd run the soles off their feet and still weren't good enough to make the team. I suppose it would be easier if everyone I cut was a poor player who did not work hard, but such is seldom the case."

In his first year of coaching, Wood posted a list of the players who'd made the team. In retrospect he thinks such a method was "the chicken's way" of completing this difficult task. Later in his career Wood would talk to each young man who'd tried out for the team. He'd thank them for their efforts and explain what he thought they needed to do to improve enough to make the team.

With less than a month to prepare for their first game, Wood decided against teaching the Hinkle System. He thought such a scheme might be too difficult for the kids to learn. He opted instead to use a simple offense with a few options for getting the ball in low. In retrospect he admits that this was probably a mistake. "There's so much that you learn on the job and I learned a lot in my first year. In our first nine games we won two and lost seven. I probably lost three or four of those games just by being outfoxed by some old foxes! Not teaching the Hinkle system from the start was a mistake. I'd spent a year learning it and I didn't think I could teach it to the kids before the start of the season. We spent a lot of time on fundamentals and ran a simple pattern with a few options. We were competitive until the opposition started scouting us and from there they took some things away from us. After those first nine games, I decided that we'd better get a continuity approach or the season was going to be a long one.

"The boys learned the Hinkle system quicker than I imagined and when we started using it we started winning. After that 2-7 start we ended the season at 10-11. The boys had learned the system and could run it well. At the end of the season some of our young men wanted to know why we hadn't started the season using that offense and I had to confess that I thought they'd be 'snowed under' by it. Anyway, I learned early that young ballplayers can adjust to things that maybe I didn't think they could handle."

The Red Devils faced Hardinsburg in Marvin's coaching debut in the Indiana State Basketball Tournament. He started Glen "Lefty" Jacobs and Roy "Junior" Flick at guards; Jack Beatty and Frank Marshall filled the forward slots; and Blaine Hendrix started at center. His first sectional contest was a wild and wooly affair that went back and forth through four periods. At the end of regulation the score stood tied at 59. In the first overtime period French Lick fell behind four points and trailed 63-61 with less than ten seconds remaining. It looked like Marvin would lose his debut, but then Frank Marshall made a quick move on his defender and hit a layup with :03 showing on the clock. The first overtime period ended with the score tied at 63.

A double overtime in 1951 was quite different than overtime periods today. While the first overtime lasted three minutes, the second was a "sudden death" period in which the first team scoring two points won the contest (sudden death overtimes were featured in high school competition from 1938 to 1961). Obviously, the team controlling the tip had a big advantage. Hardinsburg controlled the tip, but was unable to score. The Red Devils captured the rebound and when Jack Beatty hit a bucket from the corner he gave his teammates and Coach Wood a sectional victory.

The Red Devil's next opponent, Pekin, was not nearly as tough as Hardinsburg. French Lick's fastbreak quickly put Pekin in a deep hole and permitted Marvin to use his reserves, giving his battle-worn starters a breather. French Lick won that contest 47-37 and faced Marengo in a semi-final match-up.

The Marengo Cavemen proved to be too much for Wood's Red Devils. His charges played their hearts out, but came up on the short end of the 44-39 score. The loss was especially tough because Marengo hit a three-quarters-of-the-court heave at the end of the third quarter which put them ahead by two points. Had they not hit that shot, French Lick could have utilized their "stall" offense to drain away the clock and take a chance at a late-game run. Instead it was Marengo who held the ball and forced the Red Devils to commit fouls. The Cavemen hit their freethrows and Marvin's first tournament appearance came to an end.

Despite his team's sub-five hundred record and the loss in the semi-final of the sectional, Marvin thought they'd had a good season. "I felt pretty good. I think the players felt good. We'd shown improvement over those first nine games. We'd made major adjustments through the year and the team handled them well. The boys had gained a lot of confidence. At 10-11 we'd just missed having a winning season and I believe that both the fans and the players had accepted the type of program I wanted to run. I'd learned a lot, gained some confidence, and had a better idea as to what we had to do to be successful."

While Marvin wrestled with the challenges of his fledgling career, Mary Lou worked to establish their new home. Her efforts, however, were hampered by illness, making her first year away from her family and friends difficult. "When we moved to French Lick our plan was to get settled and then I would look for a job. Instead, a kidney problem I'd had during the summer recurred," recalls Mary Lou. "Being sick in a new town, knowing few people and not knowing a doctor, caused me a lot of distress. Jane Hammerling, the principal's wife, suggested I go see Dr. Sugarman, one of the doctors in town. Dr. Sugarman said I needed to see a specialist and offered to get me an appointment with one in Louisville. We didn't know anyone from Louisville so I told him that I'd rather go up to Indianapolis where I had family and friends. He was understanding and got me an appointment with a urologist at Methodist Hospital in Indianapolis. A week later I had surgery to remove the kidney which put me off my feet for almost a month."

Shortly after her surgery Mary Lou received some medical news of a more pleasant sort—she discovered she was pregnant. Her baby was due in the Spring of 1951. So, on top of the move to French Lick, the Woods were faced with yet another imminent change—an additional member to their family. In the midst of all of this, they also discovered that Marvin's salary, three hundred dollars a month, could be stretched over thirty days—but just barely. His income from teaching was less than their combined incomes when Mary Lou worked for Chevrolet and Marvin had worked on the farm or in the factory.

Forty years later, the Woods find it easy to laugh at how tough things were. "I can remember one time when we drove home (125 miles) with thirteen cents in our pockets," Mary Lou recalls. "We knew the folks would not give us money, but they would give us a tank of gas and food. We'd only use half of the gas getting back home, so we'd have half-a-tank of gas and groceries to get us through the week. We figured that this was cheaper than spending the weekend in French Lick. My mom and dad would worry about us driving back so, when we got home we'd call their house person-to-person and asked for Marvin. By doing so they'd know we were home and no one would be charged for the call."

During their first winter in French Lick, the area was hit with a rare snowfall which made driving nearly impossible. That winter, too, brought some of the coldest days in state's history. Mary Lou laughs as she relates that they'd been told time and again of the mild southern Indiana winters.

Aside from her health, the weather, and finances, Mary Lou had another major adjustment to make. She began to discover what it was like to be married to a high school basketball coach. She learned that not everybody was as enthusiastic about Marvin's coaching philosophies as she was and had to develop the ability to enjoy the game despite untoward comments about her husband. She had to learn how to deal with the nights alone when Marvin was with his team or scouting the opposition.

She confides that there have been times when she felt like she played second fiddle to a basketball, but quickly adds that she could have done a lot worse. Her relationship with Marvin has been a source of happiness and contentment. As she sees it, there are trade-offs for nearly every situation in life. "Yes, there were times when I resented the fact that he spent so much time with his teams, but I don't think anyone enjoyed those Friday and Saturday nights more than I did. I loved to watch those games. I think the wife of a coach must enjoy the sport or I don't see how they can handle it."

The Woods have known coaches who left coaching to save their marriage. Such has not been the case with them. Marvin gives Mary Lou credit for his success and often refers to her as his number-one assistant coach. "Mary Lou has been a student of the game," he relates. "She'd come over and watch us practice and knew the things we were trying to do. I've called her my number-one assistant coach because all along the way she's made criticisms and suggestions and many times she's been right."

A vocal supporter of the Red Devils, Mary Lou turned many heads in those first few years with her fierce enthusiasm for her husband's teams. In fact, during the Hardinsburg sectional game at Paoli, while pregnant with Douglas, she was so demonstrative in her support that she had to be restrained by fellow fans who feared she might fall over the edge of a balcony.

As Marvin's first year at French Lick drew to a close, he began to feel more comfortable with his job and looked forward to the birth of their first child. Mary Lou recalls those days, ". . . Dr. Sugarman delivered babies in his office and there was no way that I was going to have my baby anywhere other than in a hospital. I told (the doctor) and he said I could go to the hospital in Washington which was about thirty miles away. I didn't want to do that either. So, two weeks before my due date

I went home and stayed with my folks.

"On the night of commencement I called Marvin to tell him I'd been having labor pains. He asked how soon I thought it would be. I told him it wouldn't be for awhile yet, but I hoped he'd come up since commencement was over. He then explained that he needed to get in touch with Warren Guthrie because they were supposed to start summer baseball next week. He told me that he'd wait and come up in the morning.

"This disturbed me, but it turned out all right. Marvin always seemed to have a way of being there at the right time. My mother took me to the hospital at two o'clock in the morning and Marvin showed up at eleven the next day. I still hadn't had the baby, and then, unbeknownst to me, he and my doctor went out and watched softball games. They came back just before I had Douglas."

Despite what might appear to have been a cavalier attitude about the experience, Marvin confesses that he was as nervous and excited as any father-to-be. "I think I enjoyed having a child as much as Mary Lou did. One of the most exciting things was that our first child was a boy. He'd carry the Wood name. The baby was healthy and so was Mary Lou. We were concerned about her because of her earlier health problems, but she came through in great shape. I think having a child did a lot to tie us together even more closely. The new child also brought more visits from the grandparents which we both appreciated. I think they enjoyed Douglas almost as much as we did. It was a neat time in our lives."

* *

Marvin and Mary Lou spent the summer enjoying little Douglas, but when Fall approached Marvin was eager to get back to school and his second season with the Red Devils. Marvin discovered that he enjoyed his chosen career. He liked working with the kids and the kids seemed to enjoy him. When Marvin, whose career is full of stories about young men struggling to become adults, looks back at his years in French Lick he remembers a couple of incidents in particular.

"I can remember an incident that happened early in my first year," he recalls. "A young man named Paul Oswald played on the team and he always came into practice smelling of smoke. I confronted him one day and said he smelled like he'd been smoking. He admitted that he had been smoking and, when I started to get on him, he told me that smoking didn't hurt him in the least. I was still pretty young and full of ideas about how to confront such situations so I challenged him to run a mile. He said he'd race me a mile and he'd beat me. I may have been young, but I wasn't in too great of shape back then. We ran the mile and I was determined to beat him. I beat him, but only by about three steps. I paid the price for weeks after that—I was sore and stiff and hobbled around the house and school. I felt like I might die. I never did catch that kid smoking, but you can bet he didn't play much after that." Another player, Jack Beatty recalls that Wood caught him smoking, but handled it differently than he did with Paul. Marvin made him run one hundred laps around the gym during practice. The punishment must have worked because Beatty is quick to add that he's never again smoked a cigarette.

Wood also recalls taking a group of players to Indianapolis to see the state finals. As it turned out, one of his players intended to use that trip for different entertainment. "I encouraged our players to go to the state finals. I wanted them to get the feeling of all of the excitement with hope that it might inspire them to be better ballplayers. I tried to take as many of our boys as possible. I was always concerned about their safety and tried to take good care of them because if my son were to be with someone in similar circumstances I would want them to do the same. I kept everyone's ticket for fear that they might lose it and didn't hand them out until we were right at the fieldhouse door.

"On this occasion I'd saved the seat next to me for Dewey Lewis. He was our youngest player and I wanted to be certain that I could keep an eye on him. Shortly before the start of the game a gentleman walked up and sat in Dewey's seat. I told him he must have the wrong seat, but he showed me the ticket and explained that a young man had sold it to him right outside the door. I later found out that Dewey had sold his ticket and used the money to get into the Fox Theatre which featured a burlesque show. At the time, I had no idea where he was. I wasn't sure how to handle this development because by the time we were ready to leave he still had not come back. Finally, we left town without him.

"When we got home at one o'clock in the morning and I had to call Dewey's parents and tell them that he'd given us the slip. I felt very guilty. Fortunately, Dewey made it back to French Lick. He was back in school on Monday and I think he was mad at me for telling his parents."

* *

During Marvin's second season he began to demonstrate a philosophy of the game that would become his trademark. His teams have always tried to control the tempo of the game. Marvin realized early in his playing days that tempo was an important factor in any ball game. If he could control the tempo, then he felt his team had a excellent chance of winning. His primary tools in controlling tempo were the fastbreak, team defense, and "ball control" (or stall) offense.

"I learned as a player that even a good ballclub can get beat if it isn't able to play at its tempo. When you control the tempo, you're in charge. You can control tempo two ways—offensively and defensively. Offensively, you try to create situations that will permit your team to do the things that it wants to do while frustrating the defense; and defensively you want to try to make the opposition do the things you want them to do by interrupting their offense.

"I first learned about tempo when I was a freshman in high school. During our sectional championship, coach Furr used a stall offense. This surprised me because we generally liked to run—but we would not have won that ball game without the ball control offense. You see, he knew our opponents, too, liked to run, and figured that our chances would be better if we played at a slower pace." Wood further explains, "Sometimes you need to do the opposite, you need to run. Defense, too, can be used to throw the opposition out of sync. A full court press, switching man-to-man, and zone are tools to use in particular situations. I suppose the most important thing is to know what your team is capable of doing. Some teams simply don't have the ability to change from the fastbreak to ball control or vice-versa. I was lucky in my first years, I had good guards who could handle the ball which permitted us to do a number of things on offense."

French Lick had a narrow floor (42 feet wide instead of the regulation 50 feet). So Wood improvised a "stall" tactic which employed the use of a dribbling guard weaving his way around the top of the key while his teammates took positions down around the basket. Marvin also coached the Hinkle System, which would become his bread and butter offense for many years.

The pattern of weaving forwards and cutting guards helped give Marvin's teams continuity which discouraged taking ill-advised shots out of panic. Marvin's Red Devils, remembered by local old-timers for their dramatic stalling tactics, ran the fastbreak whenever they could. Marvin felt that the fastbreak provided easy baskets and an entertaining style of play. His two talented guards, Lefty Jacobs and Junior Flick, allowed his team to control the ball and to run the floor whenever that option was open. With these weapons in his arsenal Marvin looked forward to a successful second season.

With Jacobs and Flick at guard, Blaine Hendrix at center, and Jack Beatty and Phil Kaiser at forwards, the Red Devils dashed out to a 10-5 start. Along the way they posted victories against Marvin's mentor, Gerl Furr's Brownstown club, and a stubborn Corydon squad which refused to shoot freethrows in protest of French Lick's stall. French Lick won the contest 39-35. As the season progressed, the Red Devils began to get a reputation for grabbing a small lead and then putting the game into "the deep freeze." Their "cat-and-mouse" offense, as the papers dubbed it, gave opponents fits and delighted the fans.

"We played much better during my second season," Marvin recalls. "Junior Flick and Lefty Jacobs developed into a great guard tandem and with Blaine Hendrix, Jack Beatty, and Phil Kaiser we had a decent inside game. The team played well together. We were 10-5 a few weeks before the sectional, then a flu epidemic hit our school and many of our basketball players fell ill. In fact, in a game against Mitchell, I had to use both my varsity and junior varsity squads because we only had eleven players well enough to play."

The Red Devils, hampered by the "European flu," dropped four of their last five contests and ended the regular season 11-9. By tournament time Marvin's squad had recovered from its illness and eagerly anticipated their first sectional appearance at Huntingburg in that community's new fieldhouse. The realignment of French Lick from Paoli to Huntingburg caused controversy because the realignment placed the Red Devils in a much stronger field. Even so, French Lick did not draw one of the bigger schools for their first contest. They drew the Ireland Spuds who beat them by four points. The defeat brought an end to the Red Devils first winning season in nine years and helped bring to an end Marvin's stint as coach in French Lick.

Years later, Jack Beatty, a forward on that squad, still

remembers that bitter defeat. "We could not get used to those backboards with so much room behind 'em." Beatty recalls, "We played most of our ball games in what a lot of folks refer to as 'cracker boxes,'—gyms where the out-of-bounds line and the wall are only a few feet apart. The new gym in Huntingburg had damn near twenty feet between the basket and the wall. We knew the basket was still ten feet high, but I sure-as-hell couldn't hit it. I took six shots and didn't hit a one of them. After that I just quit shooting." Beatty was not the only Red Devil with shooting troubles that night. The Red Devils lost 36-32 in a game where neither team tried to stall.

The town was mighty disappointed about that ball game. In fact, after the Ireland loss Marvin received his first piece of "fan" mail—a postcard which read: "The team did not lose that game. The coach did." As a second year coach who had little experience with fan criticism, Wood was bothered by the message. "To receive such a message from a member of the community was a shock and it stung me," he admits. "It caused me to step back and question my ability to coach, (to question) the type of strategy that I had employed in that game, and to question the personnel I'd used. But, more importantly, I became a little disappointed in the community. After all, we'd brought them their first winner in nine seasons and had shown improvement over my two years. I wondered, if they'd start writing letters at this point, what would they be like if things got really bad?"

The loss to Ireland and the postcard were the first in a series of events that would lead Marvin out of French Lick. The next development came when Marvin asked the school board for a two-hundred dollar raise. They refused his request and instead offered him a fifty dollar raise. Wood was not at all happy with this development and began to consider his alternatives. He was hesitant to apply elsewhere because his two year record was 22-22 and he didn't figure such a record would serve him well in a search for another position. Then the superintendent of schools in French Lick told him that Bloomfield had asked permission to talk to him about coaching there. This set Marvin to thinking.

"That fifty dollar raise they offered only amounted to a buck a week, so when Mr. Chambers came back and told me about the Bloomfield position I asked him why they might be interested," Marvin recalls. "He told me they liked the way I handled my boys and they were impressed with the way my team performed. Well, right then I became a lot more interested in looking for another job. I thought that if somebody else was interested in me then there might be others."

Marvin spent the next few months applying for coaching positions around the southern and central part of the state. He applied at Bloomfield, Rushville, New Salem, his alma mater, Morristown, Fairmont, and, on the advice of his his high school coach, Gerl Furr, he applied at a small southern Indiana town, Milan. Wood interviewed with each school and created a list of his own priorities as to what he wanted in a new position.

"I didn't think I should move just to be making a move. Where ever I went I wanted good talent, more money, and a excellent facility. My old high school, Morristown, probably had the best facility, but I'd been told that it is not a good idea to go back and coach at the same place you played. A friend from college, Paul Weaver, told me that the material at Fairmont was 'better than average,'and my old high school coach had scouted Milan. He said it looked like they had some outstanding young people coming up and that a young coach ought to be looking for talent. Rushville was a bigger school, they had a good facility, great pay, but very little talent."

By late April Wood narrowed his choices to three schools. "I guess by that time I figured Milan had the most talent, Bloomfield was a close second, and Fairmont was not far behind. In the end, Milan and Bloomfield offered the most money which eliminated Fairmont from consideration. I was still asking for a few hundred more than either Bloomfield or Milan offered and I figured I'd wait to see if either of them would come up with more money before I made up my mind." Milan was the first school to offer Marvin what he'd asked for and in late Spring he and Mary Lou went there to sign a contract for the next school year.

Marvin recalls breaking the news about Milan to his boss, superintendent of schools, J.W. Chambers: "After signing the contract to go to Milan, I told the superintendent of my decision to leave and asked him if he wanted a letter of resignation. He said that he didn't think that would be necessary and wished me success at Bloomfield. When I told him I was leaving for Milan instead of Bloomfield he became upset and said, 'If you're going to leave then you're gonna leave right now!' He didn't give me permission to work the summer program and, in fact, informed me that my replacement would take care of summer baseball and basketball. So I felt like they pushed me out. Anyway, we left that night for Morristown with a bitter taste in our mouths."

The Woods spent the summer in Morristown, first living six weeks with Mary Lou's folks and then six weeks with Marvin's parents. Marvin made one last trip back to French Lick and loaded all of their belongings on a flatbed truck he'd borrowed from his uncle. He stored them in a garage until the Fall. Despite the circumstances surrounding their departure, the Woods have pleasant memories of Marvin's first two years as a coach. "We were just a couple of farm kids trying to adjust to being on our own. We'll always remember French Lick as the place where we started," recalls Marvin. "We learned a lot there, made some friends (and probably a few enemies). Mary Lou and I will always be grateful for the opportunity they gave us."

Jim Wendleman dishes off. Ron Truitt in the foreground. (Courtesy Indianapolis News)

5

Milan '52-'53:
A Brush
With Greatness

Starting five 1954 from left to right: Ray Craft, Ron Truitt, Bob Engel, Gene White and Bob Plump. (Courtesy Indianapolis News)

The summer of 1952 found Marvin and Mary Lou back in Morristown. They decided to live at home rather than moving to Milan. "That was a tough summer," Wood recalls. "After having been on our own for two years and having Douglas and another child on the way, moving back home required quite an adjustment. On the other hand, moving to Milan without knowing anyone would have been even more difficult—especially for Mary Lou.

"We spent a little time thinking about the way things had ended in French Lick and what might happen in Milan. I was concerned about the way things were going and hoped this situation of having to move back home would not become part of the routine—I was concerned about our decision to go to Milan, too. Until I had the chance to work with those kids, I could not be certain that they were as talented as I'd heard. We hoped we'd made the right move."

Years earlier, while Marvin was still in college taking lessons from Coach Hinkle, a group of talented young ballplayers at Milan's junior high school in Ripley County had a perfect season before losing in the County tournament. The group included Bobby Plump, Raymond Craft, Robert Engel, Ronald Truitt and Gene White. When these kids trudged back into the locker room after that tournament-ending upset, their coach, Marc Combs, told them that they could never beat another team simply by thinking they were better.

Before Marvin's arrival, the Milan Indians were coached by Herman Grinstead. Grinstead taught basketball with a loud voice and a sharp tongue, earning him the nickname "Snort." He'd holler and his teams would run, run, run. Herman liked the fastbreak and he hated to lose. Gene White, a junior forward when Marvin arrived, remembered Grinstead this way: "I think almost everybody liked Mr. Grinstead, but he had an explosive personality. When he lost his temper he could be a bear. He got the maximum effort out of each of us—probably through a fear factor. One way or another, he made you want to play hard for him."

The Indians had a solid ballclub during White's freshman and sophomore years. White, Craft, Engel, Plump, and Truitt spent most of their time on the reserve teams during those first two years. Then, one night during their sophomore season while getting soundly beat by cross-County rival, Osgood, Grinstead issued an ultimatum to his seven seniors at halftime—win this ball game or turn in your uniforms. The Indians lost and Grinstead found himself with seven varsity jerseys to fill. He called back two of the better seniors and gave the other five uniforms to a junior center, Jim Wendleman, a junior guard, Ralph Preble, and three sophomores, Bobby Plump, Bob Engel, and Ronnie Truitt. Grinstead coached this young squad to a County championship, avenged the earlier lost to Osgood, and gave sectional foe Batesville a battle before falling to the bigger team which went on to win the regional.

While the community's initial response to Grinstead's dismal of those five seniors had been negative, the outstanding performance of his sophomores raised the possibility of more County championships and winning seasons in the near future. Grinstead had made a risky move payoff, but soon got involved another risky venture which cost him his job.

At about the same time Marvin received that critical postcard sent in response to French Lick's loss in the Huntingburg sectional against Ireland, Herman Grinstead was dismissed from his coaching duties by Milan's Superintendent of Schools. The reasons for Grinstead's dismissal had something to do with his purchase of new varsity uniforms without the approval of the school board. This fiscal infraction, combined with other incidents involving his volatile personality, cost him his job.

The community's response to his dismissal was both immediate and negative. They liked Grinstead. Afterall, his team had won the County tourney and next year's team appeared to be the strongest from Milan in many seasons. Committees were formed, harsh words passed, but in the end the superintendent got his wish—Out with Grinstead and in with Wood. Despite all the hubbub, by the time Marvin came around to sign his contract, the local firestorm had subsided and only a slight undertow of resentment remained. So, while Marvin spent the summer in Morristown wondering if he'd made the right decision, the community of Milan, too, hoped their superintendent had made the right choice.

At summer's end Marvin and Mary Lou packed up their belongings and again headed south. Before they left Marvin's mother made a gift of all the rent money they'd paid her that summer.

The Woods rented a new home in Milan from the likeable town lawyer and "number one downtown coach," Bob Peak. School began after Labor Day and two weeks into the first semester the Woods were blessed with their second child.

"I was in Milan about two weeks then, knowing that the baby would be coming soon, I moved back with my folks," Mary Lou recalls. "Marvin came up on the weekend and was ready to go back on Sunday night. I was due anytime by then and I told him I wished he'd stay the night and then head back in the morning. Marvin felt he should get back to Milan because he had lessons to prepare and baseball practices to plan. When he left that night I felt very lonely and went up to my room and cried. Then about an hour later he came back and said he'd got to thinking that if he was in my shoes he'd want me to stay so he'd decided to come back and spend the night. I awakened the next morning with pains. At eight that morning I had Dee. I stayed in Morristown for two weeks after she was born. When I moved back to Milan the basketball season had not yet started so Marvin was around to help me in the evenings.

"I'd been impressed with Milan from the first day we saw the place. The town folks had held a clean-up-the-town campaign, so the streets were clean and the houses freshly painted. It was like moving into one of those neat little towns you sometimes see on a postcard. The move to Milan went a lot better than our first move to French Lick. I had a couple of weeks to get settled before the baby came. We'd bought our own furniture and our new home was pretty much in order before I came back with Douglas and Dee."

"We were really on top of the world," Marvin adds. "For the first time in our marriage we were living in our own house instead of in an apartment or with our parents. We were in debt, but we had new furniture and with our boy and girl we were living the American dream. It was nice."

Looking back at those first few months in Milan, Marvin describes the town's response to his replacing the popular Grinstead as "not overly friendly." He remembers that he was treated with respect, but felt pressure to produce a winning program. "I was an unknown to the community and I could appreciate their skepticism about a young coach who'd not really proven himself. I soon discovered that some folks were still a little angry with the superintendent over the dismissal of Grinstead. Even so, I think they did not want to abuse me because of something that had happened before I came. They were willing to give me a chance to be successful. I think they expected their team to play well. Let me say that I'm glad we were successful..."

During Fall baseball Marvin became acquainted with many of the young men he would later coach in basketball. His baseball team won the Ohio River Valley Conference with a 5-0 record. The confidence and enthusiasm he displayed while managing baseball helped to eliminate some of the uneasiness associated with such a young coach taking the reins of the community's most prized possession—its basketball team. The kids, too, were impressed with the way Marvin handled himself.

In turn, during the opening days of basketball practice, Marvin was impressed by his new team. "They'd been well-prepared fundamentally and much of the credit for that had to go to Herman Grinstead and their middle school coach, Marc Combs," says Marvin. "I was especially impressed with the work Combs had done with them in junior high. Not having to teach those kids the fundamentals gave me time to help them 'polish off' their skills. We reviewed the fundamentals, but spent more time working on what we wanted to do on offense and defense.

"Our team had good size and quickness and several outstanding ballplayers. This surprised me because Milan was a small school and to find so much talent at such a small school was rare. I looked forward to the season. I knew it would be a successful year, but wondered if we'd achieve as much success as the natives wanted. In fact, the president of the school board came in the gym one day and made this comment to me: 'The old coach says these guys ought to make it to the fieldhouse.' I interpreted that as pressure...

By that time I knew a little bit about the Grinstead situation and I hoped the team had put all of that behind them. I was concerned about the chemistry between myself and the team. Fortunately, those concerns were unfounded. The players and I got along well."

Under Grinstead the Indians had featured a run-and-gun style of offense with an emphasis on getting as many shots at the basket as possible. Grinstead's teams also employed a zone defense. Marvin changed a few of these things. He implemented the Hinkle system; tried to use man-to-man defense; kept the fastbreak, but introduced his team to the "cat and mouse" which eventually made them famous.

"With Grinstead we had some plays that we ran," Gene White recalls. "We tried to keep the floor balanced and usually passed into the post, rubbed the guards off the center, and looked for the first available shot. Keep the floor balanced; make sure one guy is always back; stay between your man and the basket— these were the rules by which we played. They were correct except we had no instruction as to how we were to do these things. We'd watch the older guys do it and try to pick some things up from them, or whatever.

"Then Mr. Wood came and fundamentally we did the same things, only the offense became a pattern instead of a play. The introduction of that strict pattern gave us the tools to do some of the things we were later able to accomplish. Aside from that he taught us how to 'screen out' for rebounds and how to run the floor with the fastbreak, In fact, the first rule for us on offense was to run the break."

Although Marvin had planned to scrap the zone defense he'd been forced to use in French Lick in favor of man-to-man, which he felt more comfortable coaching, his plans quickly changed and he was back to the zone by halftime of his first game. "I'd played man-to-man defense in college and I'd tried to use it as often as I could at French Lick," he explains. "I'd planned to do the same at Milan, but abandoned that hope by halftime of our first game. We weren't getting the job done on defense, so I tried the zone. By using it we took away their offense and won by twenty-four points."

Behind the outstanding play of Bobby Plump and Bob Engel the Indians raced out to a 9-1 start. Their only loss came to Vevay by a 56-54 score. In winning those nine games Wood's charges averaged fifty-five points while giving up only thirty nine. After that great beginning Milan lost its next two games, first to Aurora, and then to Lawrenceburg. In the stands for the Lawrenceburg defeat was Clarence Kelly who'd been hired to assist Marvin with the freshman and junior varsity squads.

Kelly, who'd recently come home from the Korean war, made the following observations: "Gene White played a terrible game that night, but aside from that I saw a lot of ability. Marvin impressed me as being positive, energetic. He had a plan. I don't know what had gone on during those first ten games, but as I got involved I found it interesting to see how well Marvin planned each practice. He was a fine Christian gentlemen deeply involved in getting his team to perform to the best of its abilities. I wasn't too keen about going to this small town in southern Indiana. But it wasn't long before I realized that I'd stumbled onto a great opportunity."

With Kelly on board, Marvin was able to devote more attention to his varsity squad and by the time the County tournament rolled around the Indians had a respectable 11-3 record and entered the tournament as the favorites.

Of course, the season was not without its more difficult moments, Bobby Plump remembers one incident that caused him a great deal of difficulty. "Towards the middle of the season, I think coach Wood thought some of us might be breaking his training rules," Plump relates. "Elizabethtown, a suburb of Cincinnati, is only about thirty miles from Milan and I think coach suspected that some of his players had been going there to party and stay out late. I'm sure that some of the guys were doing that, but I was not one of them. Anyway, he'd made this rule that we had to be in by ten on the weekdays and by midnight on weekends, but he'd never really checked us. Then, after our last practice before the New Year Holiday, he sat us down in the bleachers while he sat on a basketball out in the middle of the floor. He said, 'Tell you what, I know that some of you have not been following my training rules. Even so, I know you all want to go out on New Year's Eve and I think you should. You've worked hard and you deserve to have a good time, but here's the deal-you have to be in by 1 a.m. No later, and were going by my watch.' He told us what time he had on his watch and he promised that he'd check-up on each and every one of us.

"He said, 'Afterall, there's nothing you can't do before 1 a.m. that you can do after.' I went out on a double date that night to Versailles and we left ourselves just enough time to get back to Milan, but on the way home we had a flat tire. We changed it about as fast as they do in Indy 500' and got back home at about five minutes to one. We stayed out in the car studying for a test or something. Then, at a little after one, I saw Marvin's car drive by. The thought crossed my mind that I ought to go in the house, but I figured I was at home and that would be enough.

"Unfortunately, Marvin thought otherwise. He parked his car and walked up to our car. 'Bob,' he said, 'what time do you have?' I told him that my watch showed one o'clock. 'Well,' he said, my watch says five after and were going by my watch.' I told him that we'd had a flat tire and even offered to show it to him, but he would have nothing of it. He told me that I should have planned for that and to see him before the next game.

"He'd told us in that earlier discussion that if he caught us out past one we were going to be kicked off the team for three games. He never said anything more until the last practice before our next game. At the end of practice he told me to come in early the next day and talk to him. When I came in his first words to me were: 'Bob, I think I need to make an example out of you.' I knew right then I was in trouble. He said, 'You can't play tonight, you can't dress tonight, in fact, I want you up in the stands.'

"After I dried my tears I went up in the stands and sat down. Then, about ten minutes later, our starting center, Jim Wendleman, came up and sat next to me. I thought maybe he'd come up in support of me or something so I asked him, 'Jim what are you doing up here?' He answered, 'He got me at two o'clock Bob.'"

Marvin benched two of his best players to make a point, but with the County tournament coming the next week he gave them the alternative of running one hundred laps or the remaining two-game suspension. Of course, Plump and Wendleman ran the laps.

Wood recalls discipline was never a problem and nobody was more surprised than he to find his two of his best players out past curfew. "I knew for certain that another one of my players had not been training, but he managed to outlast me," Wood laughs as he recalls that night. "His garage door was open with the car gone at about 3:30 in the morning. But poetic justice reigned in that case because that player ended up with a sprained ankle and was unable to play anyway." Regarding his lifting of the three game suspension, Marvin himself had once been disciplined for missing a curfew. He also knew that it would be difficult to win the County tournament without Plump and Wendleman. Given the emphasis within a smaller community on winning such a tournament, Wood, his point firmly etched in the minds of his players, was not about to tackle the task without them.

Before consolidation, County tournaments were almost as important as the sectionals. Afterall, small schools generally did not fare well in the statewide tournament and the main social sphere for most small towns was centered upon the County. Ripley County provided a good example of what basketball was like before consolidation. The towns of Cross Plains, Holton,

Milan, Osgood, Napoleon, New Marion, Sunman, and Versailles comprised the eight communities involved in the Ripley County tournament. Each town was fiercely proud of their high school team and provided leather-lunged support at all of their ball games. Whenever an opponent was from one of the surrounding communities this support would become even more vocal.

Not unlike Marvin's home community, Morristown, Milan was a farming community with little in the way of entertainment outside of a few bars and a dilapidated movie theatre. Basketball was THE major form of recreational activity. Given the stature of basketball in these small towns, it was of paramount importance for a team to be successful within their County. Many coaches had lost their jobs despite having winning seasons based solely upon the fact that they had not beaten a cross-County rival. Fortunately, this would not become the case for Marvin.

Showing a portend of things to come, Milan "blew out" Sunman (59-30), Napoleon (51-33), and Versailles (68-45) to run away with the County championship for the second consecutive year. The Indian's fastbreak and stifling zone defense was too much for their Ripley County opponents. The dominance of Marvin's squad had folks in southern Indiana wondering—how good were the fastbreaking Indians?

Then, just before the sectionals, at about the time opponents had figured out how to handle Marvin's fastbreaking and pattern offenses, he threw them a change-up. In Milan's regular season finale against Osgood, they demonstrated that they could do something more than just score quickly and play defense. Leading at the end of one quarter 26-10, the Indians controlled the second canto tip, came down the court and went into a complete stall—which amounted to little more than Plump holding the ball under his arm out on the perimeter while his teammates spread out over the floor. The Cowboy defenders stayed in their zone. Nothing more than calisthenics by players trying to stay loose was accomplished until the two minute mark when Plump made a dribble drive to the basket and hit a layup. Milan scored seven points in the quarter and Osgood's Cowboys scored five. The score at halftime was 33-15.

In the second half Milan first used their "cat and mouse" offense, a Marvin Wood invention that emphasized finding a defender's "blind spot." By the end of the game their opponent's worst fears had been realized—Osgood had only touched the ball three times in the second half and had not scored a single point! Osgood, a team that one year ago had beat the Indians by thirty-six points, was unable to score a single point in sixteen minutes of play.

Word of this new weapon in Milan's arsenal quickly spread around the County. With the sectional less than a week away, opposing coaches scrambled to find a way to countermand Milan's ability to control tempo.

In the sectionals the Indians dominated their opponents. Alternating between the fastbreak and the "cat and mouse," they blitzed Osgood 51-23. In the semi-final Holton tried to give them a dose of their own medicine and stalled for most of the first half. This strategy failed because whenever the Warhorses finally did try to get a bucket Milan's stiffling zone was more than they could handle. Milan won that game 27-15.

The championship game against Batesville was close until the third quarter when Milan broke out to a ten point lead. They started the fourth with ball control and Batesville countered by fouling. By the end of the period the Indians had connected on ten freethrows and one bucket from the field. Batesville could only manage seven points, giving Milan a 42-27 victory and the school's first sectional championship since 1946.

Marvin's formula for victory was simple: run the fastbreak early and often; play good defense; and then salt away the victory with the possession offense. Each victory came as the result of a season-long emphasis on ". . . doing the little things that make a difference." Like a mechanic fine-tuning a racecar, Marvin had made adjustments all along the way. The "Cat and Mouse" offense and zone defense were two such examples.

"The possession or cat and mouse offense we used at Milan was different than the one I'd coached at French Lick," Wood explains. "At Milan we started with one person out at the center circle, two players on opposite sides of the court at the top of the circle, and two players on opposite sides on the baseline. We wanted the ball in the center of the court because it made it more difficult for teams to double team the ballhandler. The man handling the ball would pass it to one side or the other and then cut towards the basket. We coached our players not to run between their defender and the ball on their way to the basket. We did this because as our player headed for the basket there would always be one second when the defender would be unable to see both the ball and the person he was guarding. The key to the offense was to get the ball to the cutting player at that moment. We kept the floor balanced, made sure our passes led the receiver, and always hit the open man in case of a double team.

"The offense forced the defenders to stay alert. With our quickness little could be done to take the ball away from us. Our opponent's only hope was that we'd make an error or miss a shot—but we worked hard at getting good shots and not making turnovers."

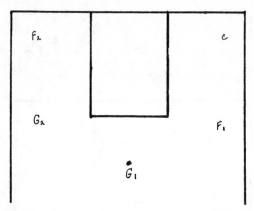

Cat and Mouse or Give & Go-Fig. 1: - 1. Basic Philosophy-Balanced floor.
2. Prevent the double team.
3. Create one on one opportunities.

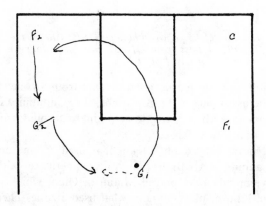

Fig. 2. G1 passes to G2 and cuts to basket away from the pass. F2 moves up to balance the floor.

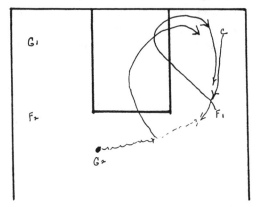

Fig. 3. G2 dribbles to mid court, F1 cuts back door to the basket, C moves up for pass from G2, G2 cuts to the basket away from the pass.

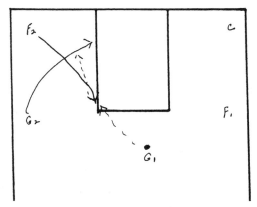

Fig. 4. G2's defense is overplaying G2, F2 cuts to the ball for pass from G1, G2 cuts back door to basket for pass from F2.

Knowing his team played great defense from a zone, Marvin sought the assistance of Marc Combs, the community's junior high school basketball coach, to help him better understand the dynamics of a zone defense.

"I had never played on a team that used a zone defense," Marvin admits. "At Butler my only experience with zone defense came when we played Miami of Ohio, which was the only team I'd ever played against that used a zone. There were many things I did not understand about such a defense. You can play a zone many different ways. After working with Marc I learned his reasons for using a zone and discovered that his objectives were similar to mine with the man-to-man.

"We wanted to make opponents shoot from the perimeter. Their percentage was not going to be nearly as good from 15-18 feet as it was from 12 feet and in. We thought there were certain areas from which particular opponents shot well. We wanted to take those areas away from them without conceding anything inside. After a shot we stressed 'blocking out' within the perimeter. Rebounding is difficult for teams playing a zone and we wanted to turn that around. So, we had a lot of little things that we wanted to do in our zone that were a lot like man-to-man. In fact, we often played a zone where each player played the person in their zone man-to-man."

The Indian's sectional victory was a pleasant but not completely unexpected event. Batesville, the perennial powerhouse in the Ripley County sectional, had not had a great season and the other County teams did not have the talent found on the Milan ballclub. On the other hand, winning at the Rushville regional would require an extraordinary effort. In fact, winning the regional would require a a lot of luck—maybe even a miracle . . . A miracle was exactly what Marvin and his Indians received.

Trailing 45-36 to an inspired Knightstown Morton Memorial team with only 1:35 remaining in the fourth quarter, Marvin had his players press the Mortons all over the floor. With the score 45-37 Bobby Plump stole the inbounds pass and was immediately fouled. He converted both freethrows cutting the Memorial lead to six points with 1:17 left on the clock. Shortly thereafter, Gene White stole a long pass and hit a driving Plump with a pass which Bobby converted into an easy layup making it 45-41.

Morton then lost the ball on a travelling call and again Milan converted—this time on a layup by Ray Craft who'd come into the game in place of Bob Engel. Meanwhile, up in the stands and down along the scorers table folks could be seen pointing at the scoreboard. Apparently, in the midst of Milan's frantic comeback attempt, the scorer had failed to turn on the clock.

Oblivious to this critical error Memorial cautiously brought the ball upcourt hoping to add to their slim two point lead. At Memorial's end of the court Ron Truitt committed his fifth personal foul. Knightstown hit both freethrows to push the Memorial lead back up to four points with :45 remaining.

The Indians quickly came downcourt and got another layup from Plump. On the other end Plump committed a foul and Memorial's Wheeler hit both freethrows making the score 49-45. At :25 Bill Jordan who'd subbed for the fouled-out Truitt was fouled and converted both of his freethrows. Trailing by two points with time running out, the Indians continued to press all over the floor which eventually caused Morton Memorial to panic. Gene White intercepted an errant pass, found Ray Craft open, and Craft hit the bunny to send the game into overtime.

Milan controlled the overtime tip and Craft scored again giving the Indians a 51-49 lead. The two point lead held until Knightstown hit two free throws and sent the game into a second "sudden death" overtime. Milan again controlled the tip. When Gene White missed a layup Memorial covered the rebound and it looked like Milan was finished—But Memorial could not convert. The game ended on Milan's next possession when Plump drew a foul on a drive to the basket. He hit both freethrows giving Milan a 53-51 victory.

"I don't think anyone in our crowd knew we could win the game with two freethrows. They thought the sudden death rule meant that the team had to score a basket." Mary Lou recalls, "I'd known from our sectional in French Lick that the rule was two points. So, when Plump hit those freethrows I knew we won. Anyway, I found myself, and to this day I'm not exactly sure how this happened, but I went out across the court and found myself in the arms of a three-hundred-pound news reporter, Tiny Hunt. One of the most embarrassing things I ever had to do was to walk back across that floor to our cheering section."

The stopped clock played a major role in Milan's victory. The Indianapolis News reported that twenty-eight seconds passed before this error was corrected. Had it not been for those precious twenty-eight seconds, the Indians would have been heading for home instead of into the evening's contest against tenth-ranked Connersville.

The Indians did not have long to savor their community's first-ever regional victory. The nightcap against Connersville would require all of the energy and concentration they could muster. Fortunately, they broke out to a 6-0 lead against the talented Spartans. Up 8-4 Milan went into its patented "cat and mouse." Connersville would have none of this and "circled the wagons" down around the basket. Undaunted, Plump stood out at the centerline for four minutes doing nothing more than occasionally switching the ball from one hand to the other while his teammates swung their arms and ran in place to stay limber. Connersville's fans, angered by this strategy, began to boo and hiss. Eventually they started throwing coins at the Milan bench and later some could be seen spitting and shouting expletives at Marvin and his charges. Amid this rude barrage the first period ended with Milan up 8-4.

Milan grabbed the second quarter tip and went back into their stall. They held the ball until the last :45 of the quarter when Plump made a dash for the basket, pulled up below the circle and hit a beautiful jump shot sending the Indians into the lockerroom at halftime with a 10-4 lead.

In a clever attempt to thwart the Indians' stalling tactics, Connersville came out after halftime and pressed all over the floor. Little by little the Spartans worked their way back into the game cutting Milan's lead to 17-15 by the quarter's end.

Connersville then scored the first three points of the fourth quarter to take the lead for the first time in the game. The two teams traded baskets until Connersville pulled ahead 22-20 with 2:21 left in the game. At the 1:10 mark Ray Craft hit a layup to tie. Bob Engel then stole a Spartan pass allowing Craft to hit another bucket putting the Indians up by two. Connersville had a chance to tie but missed the shot. Ronnie Truitt cornered the rebound and held until the claxon blared. The Indians, aided by the timer and the budding genius, Marvin Wood, had won the school's first regional crown.

Looking back Marvin counts the victory against Connersville as one of the sweetest in his career. "I can remember my brother-in-law coming up to me before th game to tell me he didn't think we had a chance against Connersville. Connersville was sleek. They'd been ranked in the top ten all year and there we were just a bunch of country kids. There was no way that we were going to be able to run with them. But on the first rebound of the game I knew that we would be able to play with them. Our center, Jim Wendleman, was a big ole' farm boy and he grabbed the ball with both hands, got his elbows flapping and knocked three Connersville ballplayers right on their butts—and I mean he flattened 'em! Well, that did a little something to their confidence and Jim Wendleman owned the boards after that.

"Leading 8-4 we went into our ball control offense. I thought they'd try to stop us from doing this, but Connersville thought they could beat us any time and any way they wanted. As we were holding the ball, I figured we had a good chance of beating them because they were over-confident. In fact, there were times when I was more worried about the crowd's reaction. They cussed us, threw coins at us, and, late in the game, they even came by our bench and spit all over us.

"That was probably one of my most rewarding victories—just because of the way their fans treated us. After the game we were in the locker room talking about how they'd treated us when one of our guys piped up and said, 'Yea, but we beat the livin' liver out of 'em. We won the game and they're out of it.' We gained a world of confidence and solidarity from that ball game."

The community went bonkers over the Indian's first-ever regional title. Bill Steinmetz, a local businessman who'd played on a sectional winner back in '46, came running into the showers with his suitcoat and tie to hug Plump. The success of the basketball team was like a fairy tale. Most of the talk around Milan was now centered on the trip to "the big barn" in Indianapolis.

When the team arrived back in Milan, the town wanted to parade them around a-top a fire engine but Marvin would have nothing of this. His boys were still in the tournament and he saw no point in resting on the past week's accomplishments. This, too, was his first venture into the semi-finals and he was keen on making a good showing.

"That week went by so fast that I can hardly remember what happened," Marvin admits. "I do remember the scouting report on our next opponent, Attica. We were going to have to play a smart ball game to beat them. It pleased me to see our boys had not let winning go to their heads. They came into practice and worked as hard as they had all season. In some ways I knew we weren't all that good, but on the other hand these kids had something special. The chemistry was there."

In Milan's first trip to the Semi-Finals, the Indians, Attica, Shelbyville, and Crispus Attucks provided spectators with some of the most exciting basketball the state has ever seen. The afternoon contest, featuring Milan and Attica, was a nip and tuck affair. The lead changed hands throughout the game with Milan leading early by as many as seven. Fighting back from a 20-13 deficit, Attica forged a 26-25 lead. At halftime the score was 29-29.

Neither team could pull away in the third, ending the stanza with Milan in front 41-39. When Attica's Bill Sisk started the final canto by hitting two freethrows Milan went into its "cat and mouse" and slowly pushed the game along until the 3:10 mark. With the score tied at 45, Plump tucked the ball under his arm at center court and let the clock tick down to 2:29. At that point the Indians started looking for a shot, but could find none they wanted to take. At :06 Plump tried a drive at the basket but lost the ball as time expired.

The overtime period began with Attica controlling the tip. They took a shot but were unable to score. Milan got the rebound, came down to their end of the court, and went into their ball control offense. Plump broke for a layup, but missed it. Fortunately, Gene White tipped it in and gave Milan a 47-45 lead. Attica's Paul Sullivan hit one of two freethrows on the other end. Plump got a similar opportunity for Milan, but missed both shots. On the second miss Gene White again cornered the rebound and was promptly fouled. Gene hit both attempts expanding Milan's lead to 49-46. Attica hit a layup as time expired, but the Indians walked off with a 49-48 victory.

Attica's Bill Sisk had a spectacular game, scoring 21 points and collaring numerous rebounds. The Milan attack was paced by Bob Engel, Gene White, and Bobby Plump. As Marvin's squad dressed and headed out for a meal and a nap, they fully expected to face Crispus Attucks, the state's top-ranked team, in the evening's finale. Such would not be the case, however, as Shelbyville's Bears pulled off a stunning upset. They beat Attucks 46-44 in a thrilling ball game. The Bears had trailed until the fourth quarter when they rallied behind the efficient inside play of Jim Plymate, and the accurate outside shooting of Tom Taylor. Slowly erasing a seven-point deficit, the Bears pushed ahead late in the game. With the score tied at 44 and time running out, Attucks' Hallie Bryant drove towards the bucket and was assessed with what later would be described as "a questionable offensive foul." Plymate hit both freethrows and time expired before Attucks could take another shot.

Shelbyville's victory over Attucks almost became the biggest upset in the state that day. The biggest upset, however, came later that night when Milan completely demoralized the Golden Bears. In one of the strangest ball games in state basketball history, Milan set a defensive record that will never be broken.

They held Shelbyville to only two field goals for the entire game! The Bears took 42 shots, but could only connect on 2 of them. Shelbyville's futility from the field was compounded by Milan's "give and go" (a more accurate name for the "cat and mouse" offense used by Angelo Angelopolous in the Indianapolis News), which led the Indians to a shocking 43-21 victory.

Unable to find the range from outside nor penetrate the Indians 2-1-2 zone from the inside, Shelbyville was never in the ball game. Gene White, who made the All Semi-Final team remembers the game this way: "I think that might have been the best game we ever played. I remember the first shot their center took. He was a tall, sleek black kid and he made this beautiful move beneath the basket and laid the ball up on the other side. Well, our big farm boy, Jim Wendleman took a flying leap at that shot and just smashed it against the backboard. I'm tellin' you, it was the best damn defensive play he ever made. You could see their center's shoulders sag and I don't think he took but two or three more shots the rest of the night. I'll grant you that they were tired after playing against Attucks, but I don't think they had any idea how to attack our zone. And Plump, well he could do just about anything he wanted. At about that time I began to realize that it wasn't just our guys in practice who couldn't stop him. He had a head-and-shoulders fake that simply froze his defender. By the time the defender reacted Plump was already past him and heading to the basket. But it wasn't just Plump on offense either—it was teamwork with a capital T."

Wood agrees that his team played well, but he also saw a Shelbyville team that had played their hearts out in the afternoon contest. "A lot of our success could be contributed to Crispus Attucks," he admits. "Shelbyville had played a tough ball club in the afternoon. In fact, I think they'd been mentally prepared to play Attucks. I don't know if they'd planned to go any further than that. I must say they had great success against Attucks, but when it came time to play us they had to change their game plan. I think they were emotionally and physically drained and thus, were unable to make the adjustments needed to compete with us.

"They'd prepared for one game, they'd played their one game—and that was it. Of course, if you'd ask Frank (Frank Barnes, coach of Shelbyville) I'd like to think that he'd tell you he lost because of the 'Wood jinx.' My brother John had been a nemesis to him in high school. In fact, I don't think he ever beat a team with a 'Wood' associated with it . . . We just played our game and when they couldn't hit the bucket, well, that just helped us gain more confidence as the game wore on."

Action from 1953 semi-final versus Shelbyville Bears. Bobby Plump drives against Shelbyville. (Courtesy Indianapolis News)

On the way home from the Semi-Final championship, Wood remembers thinking that they'd been more lucky than good. "It was like living in a dream world. As a coach I knew that we were not that strong. I found myself wondering: 'How in the world is this taking place?' I began to question a lot of things. You see, I'd always thought that talent and hard work were all that was required. But I was finding out that the bounce of the ball or the luck of the draw made all the difference in the world. A lot of good things were happening for us. We were getting some lucky bounces and the draw, especially in the semi-final, seemed to be in our favor."

Back home in Milan the community struggled to get a little bit of work done in between long conversations about their state-final-bound Indians. The town board proclaimed the next Saturday, 21 March, to be a local holiday. Throughout Ripley County an excitement here before unknown could be seen in the faces, or heard in the conversations of folks from Holton to Versailles. One woman wrote to the Osgood Journal and described the sensation as ". . . being caught in the middle of a dream and yet when I pinch myself I find that I am very much awake." The sportswriters, especially, enjoyed the team's success. Marvin had a winsome personality and his deprecating evaluation of his team's abilities was a welcome relief from the smug self-confidence often found in the coaching fraternity.

Little Milan had caught the fancy of an entire state and when they headed back to Indianapolis it is safe to say that every small town from Whiting to Watson was pulling for the Indians.

Milan drew South Bend Central in the afternoon's first contest. South Bend, coached by Elmer McCall, had Paul Harvey, one of the state's best guards. The rest of the team was both tall and quick. They completely outclassed Milan. From opening tip to the final gun, Milan was never in the ball game.

Unlike Shelbyville, these Bears were red hot from the field and jumped out to a 13-7 lead. By halftime they expanded that lead to 25-14. The Indians were cool from the field and, unlike in their earlier contests, unable to control the offensive boards. The eventual state champs continued to hammer away at their smaller, less-accurate opponents, running away with a 56-37 victory—no overtimes, no generosity from the timer, and no stalling with the lead, just a plain old-fashioned trip to the woodshed. The nineteen point deficit was the largest margin of defeat a Wood-coached team had experienced. And for Marvin, coming on the heels of the tremendous victory one week earlier, it was a difficult pill to swallow.

"All I could think was: Here's another small town team flubbing it in the final four with the whole state watching. I was disappointed with our play. I didn't think we were mentally prepared at the start of that game. We'd had some shenanigans at the hotel on the night before the game, then one of our kids had his hand slammed in the trunk of a car on the way over to the gym, and Plump hurt himself during the warmups. When the game started we got behind right away and it simply got worse from there.

"... I knew that we'd won a few games along the way that we probably should not have won, but I also felt that if we'd been able to play man-to-man defense we might have been able to

Shelbyville center Phillips attempts a shot over Wendleman. Gene White (left), Ron Truitt (middle), Bobby Plump and Bob Engel position themselves for a rebound. (Courtesy Indianapolis News)

contain South Bend's excellent perimeter shooting . . . Unlike
Connersville or Shelbyville, Central had a week to prepare for
us. They had more quickness and talent than anyone we'd
played. They used those assets in a way that stopped us from
doing the things we wanted to do. We were big in '53, bigger
than most people remember, but compared to South Bend we
were also kinda slow. They took advantage of that. I was
disappointed that we lost, but very pleased with the way our
boys had conducted themselves throughout the season and
during the tournament. It had been a great year."

Paul Harvey heads down court after a Milan turnover.

South Bend Central vs. Milan 1953 State Final (afternoon game): Jim Wendleman follows in a missed freethrow against the South Bend Central Bears.

After the game Wood addressed his teary-eyed team, congratulating them on an excellent year and blaming himself for the loss against Central. "We were all sitting there feeling mighty low and then coach Wood asked for our attention," Bob Engel recalls. "He said: 'We've come a long this year and we've accomplished a lot. I'll take this loss as my fault.' He said, 'We don't have but one defense, but I'll guarantee you that next year we will have it all. Unfortunately, we're going to lose a couple of good ballplayers, but we've had a good year, an excellent year, and I'm proud of you guys.'"

When the team arrived back in Milan they were met by over two thousand supporters. On Sunday the town had a parade for the team and later, in front of the high school, Marvin, Mary Lou, and many of Milan's leading citizens gave inspiring speeches. The boys on the team enjoyed this display of appreciation, but all were disappointed that they'd gone so far and yet got nothing in the way of silver or gold for their efforts. "We'd gotten just far enough not to get anything," Ray Craft recalls. "Back in those days only the runner-up and the champions got rings. If you lost in the afternoon, you went home with nothing."

Perhaps the silver-lining in that loss to South Bend Central was the play of Bobby Plump. He made first-team All State that year and was on the All State-Final team. His 19 point performance against Central gave him a tremendous boost in confidence. "Despite the problems we'd had, I felt very comfortable and had a helluva ball game. Don't get me wrong, nobody was more unhappy about that loss than I was, but when I walked off of that floor I knew I could play with anybody.

1953 State Finalist Team. Mascot David Jordan. Row 1 left to right: Cheerleader Joan Johnson, Virginia Voss, Bob Engel, Bob Plump, Ron Truitt, Jim Wendleman, Gene White, Eleanor Voss Brinkman. Row 2: Asst. Coach Kelly, Jim Call, Bill Jordan, Ralph Preble, Ray Craft, Ken Wendleman, Roger Schroder, Jim Smith, Coach Wood.

"I don't say that to brag and it wasn't that I didn't have confidence before, but until that game I didn't really know my capabilities. I had no idea what I could do ... They were as easy for me to score against as anybody we'd played and they were a talented team. People talk about 'players coming into their own,' or whatever. Well, after that game I knew that I could be a excellent player, maybe one of the best in the state—it was through the heat of competition that I came to that realization."

On the morning after their loss in the state finals, Marvin and Mary Lou talked about the season and all that had come to pass. Marvin was especially pleased with the development of Bobby Plump. But his thoughts were mainly centered upon how close they'd come to the goal he'd coveted ever since that first sectional championship back in Morristown. "You know dear," Marvin remembers telling his wife, "that might be the closest we ever come to winning a state championship."

"I know," Mary Lou replied, "but it was fun and if that's all the closer we get, well then, its a lot closer than most other folks have been."

6

Milan '53-54: The "Miracle" Season

By the time school let out for summer break, most of the fervor over the successful basketball season had subsided. The boys were involved in summer jobs and farm chores while their parents and community worked hard to pay the bills. Marvin, who'd received a nice raise for his efforts, found summer employment with Seagram's in Lawrenceburg where he worked in plant security. His team's success made him a celebrity and he received plenty of praise from his co-workers. Aided by the raise and the money he would earn at the distillery, Marvin purchased a brand new '53 Pontiac from the Volz dealership which had provided vehicles for the ballclub during the state tournament.

He and Mary Lou were beginning to see some of the benefits from the decisions they'd made in the earlier years. "Yes, that was a good Summer," Marvin recalls. "I received a raise from the school board and, with the job at Seagram's, I made more money then I had in any previous summer. Of course, my co-workers offered plenty of advice as to what I should do in the coming season and I played a lot of basketball with people from work.

"Mary Lou and the kids were healthy and happy and it was pleasant to come home to my family at a reasonable hour each day. I must admit that our successful season helped to make the summer a lot more fun. Even so, I was looking forward to the challenges of the next year."

Regarding the coming season, Marvin knew his team would not be as tall—but they would be a little bit quicker. Before school had let out, he'd talked to Bob Engel about changing from a guard to a forward. Engel, impressed that his coach would come to him asking a favor, remembers that conversation. "He came to me and said, 'Bob I'm going to ask you to do me a favor. I can't tell you to do this, but if you'll listen I think you'll see that what I'm asking makes a lot of sense. We lost a couple of our taller players and next year you're going to be one of the tallest guys on the team—would you consider playing forward instead of guard?' I told him if he wanted me to play forward I'd do my best to play forward. I spent the summer working on pick-and-roll, screening out, and playing with my back to the bucket. I worked harder because the coach asked me to do this rather than telling me. Marvin was that kind of coach. He made you want to be the best you could be."

The unique relationship between Marvin and his players had

played an important role in the '53 season and would continue to be an asset in '54. The players trusted Marvin's judgement. They did what he told them to do. Marvin, on the other hand, listened to his players and tried to provide thoughtful answers to their questions. While it was always understood that he was in charge, his players made suggestions and expressed their opinions on how certain situations should be handled. "... This is what I mean when I talk about chemistry---those kids and I thought alike," Marvin explains. "For example, when I called a time out because the opponent's defense had been over-playing us they'd come over to the bench I could hear them talking about what might work to beat that defense. A lot of times I would hear them mention the same play I intended to call—we always seemed to be on the same page."

The chemistry between the coaches, too, was good. Marc Combs, who'd worked with these young men in grade school and junior high, stressed the same fundamentals Marvin continued to stress when he took over for Grinstead. Combs tried to teach his players to treat every practice and every game as a learning experience. Such an approach laid the groundwork for Marvin's intense practice sessions. One of the fundamentals Combs taught the boys was to be be effective rebounders. "Down in the lower grades I always tried to teach the boys that a small player can out rebound a taller one, but only if he's in the proper position," Marc explains. "If Marvin had not continued to stress the importance of blocking-out for rebounds, the smaller team in '54 would have been in a lot of trouble." Of course, Marvin knew how important it was to block-out from his days as a player. He was pleased to discover that his players already understood this principle as it was a critical factor in the success of their zone defense.

One of the biggest liabilities of a zone defense is its vulnerability on rebounds. Teams employing a zone are often victimized by second or third shots at the bucket. This comes as a result of not having a body on the rebounder. Marvin and Marc countered this liability by teaching a zone defense which emphasized finding someone to block out as soon as a shot was taken. "I think the tendency with a lot of coaches who coach a zone is to concentrate on the defense," says Marvin. "They're hoping to cause their opponent to take a bad shot, but the defense is not complete until the ball is in your hands. Therefore, we taught our kids to guard an assigned area and to block-out a specific individual."

Wood's coaching approach to the zone defense was augmented by Gene White's outstanding ability to read offenses. "Whitey probably was the biggest factor in the success of our zone defense." Marc Combs recalls, "Playing in the middle of our 2-1-2, he directed the defense. He had the ability to see what was going to happen next and called for shifts according to what he saw."

"With Whitey in there it was like having a coach on the floor," adds Marvin. "He recognized what other teams were trying to do and he'd be right up front about what he saw and what he thought we ought to do to stop them. He could do that both offensively and defensively." White, not as athletic as some of his other teammates, got the most out of his abilities by doing exactly as he was told and by paying attention to what was happening on the court.

A smart player with limited athletic ability is not nearly enough to get a team to the state championship. White was fortunate to have talented ball players to "coach." At the top corners of the 2-1-2 zone were Bobby Plump and Raymond Craft. Both were quick and played tough defense. Waving their hands in the faces of the opposition, they would start harassing the opposing guards as soon as they crossed the center line. This tactic forced opponents to either run their offense further from the basket or attempt long passes which were easier to steal.

The lower corners of the zone were anchored by Bob Engel and Ronnie Truitt. Arms raised and ready to bat away any errant pass, Engel and Truitt would shift as the ball went from one side of the court to the other. Truitt's long arms and wide hands posed a difficult obstacle to any pass coming into the perimeter and Engel's speed and height stopped small guards from breaking for "back door" attempts at the bucket. With White in the middle directing traffic, Milan's zone became a "team defense" capable of frustrating most attempts to penetrate to the basket.

Despite the effectiveness of the zone defense, Marvin felt that his team should be able to play man-to-man too. This lesson was brought painfully to bear when South Bend Central's left-handed ace, Paul Quiggle, hit four outside shots early in the '53 state final game. Wood had promised the team they would learn to defend man-to-man. It was a promise he kept. "In my second season we practiced man-to-man defense every night, but in the games we generally used the zone," Marvin recalls. "Knowing we might one day have to use man-to-man in a game, I decided we had to convince our kids they could play it. So, one night in a ballgame against Versailles I told our players we were going to play man-to-man no matter what the consequences. We got down by several points and at the timeouts or quarter breaks the boys would come over and ask to change to a zone. I stuck to my guns and they finally got the message. They played their best man-to-man defense of the year. We won that game by eleven points."

Such was Marvin's approach to the game. He wanted this team to be able to do everything—and by the end of his second season they could. Milan could beat a team with the fastbreak, or the Hinkle system, or the cat and mouse. They could play zone defense or man-to-man and, as that second season progressed, Wood and Combs had even begun to tinker with a zone press.

The fact that a group of high school basketball players was able to do so many different things on a basketball court is a testimony to the concept of teamwork and the unique relationship between the players. Craft, Engel, Plump, Truitt, and White had been playing together since grade school and in the process they'd become as close as brothers both on and off of the court. So, while Marvin had the plan, these players had the confidence and ability to do whatever he asked of them. "By the time we were seniors we knew what we could do and we did it," explains Ray Craft. "Winning was more important to us than any individual achievements... When you're trying to win a ball game its difficult to be selfish. If you ask any of the guys I'm sure they'd tell you that win or lose it was fun to be a member of that team. We weren't cocky but then we weren't going to back away from any challenge either. We knew we were good but not so good that we couldn't be beat. Here was the catch—if you were going to beat us you had to beat every last one of us. It wasn't a situation where, if you stopped one or two of us then you had us beat. Everyone of us could score. Everyone of us could play defense..."

"When you talk about Milan team' is the key word," agrees Bob Engel. "Team with a capital 'T' and that was all there was to it. We played a lot of clubs that had more talent, but non that played as well together."

Bench players Roger Schroeder, Rollin Cutter, Ken Wendleman, Glen Butte, Ken Delap, Bill Wischman and Bill Jordan provided tough practice opponents and capable replacements for the starting five. The seven bench players were competitive and focused, too, on winning a state championship.

Ethan Jackson, a star guard for the neighboring Holton "War Horses" and, more recently, a successful businessman in Indianapolis, remembers playing against Milan. "I enjoyed playing against them because they almost always played a perfect game. I was quick, and against most teams I could get points by driving the lane. In fact, I don't think I played in a game where I felt the guy guarding me could stop me from going to the basket. But Milan would always frustrate me with their zone. Ray, Bobby, and Roger Schreoder were quick, but I could still get around them. The problem in driving against Milan was, if you got by one guy, another one would get in your path. If I stopped dribbling Truitt, Engel, and White would surround me with those long arms . . . There was no way one good player or two or three good players could beat them because they had five or six talented players and they played well together."

The 1953-54 Indians were 7-0 by Christmas break. In that seven game stretch they defeated: Rising Sun (52-36), Vevay, who'd beat them in '53, (65-41), Osgood, in a game that set a new attendance record for Tyson Auditorium (36-31), Seymour (61-43), Brookville, in a game where Brookville tried to stall and failed (24-20), Hanover (67-36), and Lawrenceburg (50-41).

By virtue of their fabulous year in '53 and Marvin's association with Frankfort's head basketball coach, Marvin Cave, Milan received an invitation to the Frankfort Holiday Tournament, which was to be played over Christmas break. The invitation was quite an honor for the little school whose tourney opponents would include Fort Wayne North, Frankfort, and Columbus.

Milan drew Frankfort in the opening round. Frankfort, coached by Marvin's good friend and another Hinkle protege, Marvin Cave, featured the Hinkle system and a tough man-to-man defense. The Hot Dogs got out to an early lead against Marvin's cold-shooting Indians and continued to expand their lead through three quarters. Then in the fourth quarter Milan came out in a half-court zone press. Wood and Combs had tinkered with the idea of a pressing zone for quite some time. What they'd come up with were two zone presses.

One involved a half-court trap where two defenders "trapped" the opponent at the center line. Using the center line as a third defender, the other three defenders patrolled the passing lanes. The other zone press was a simple extension of their regular press covering from baseline to baseline. The premise being that the offense would be more prone to make long, dangerous passes when confronted with a zone from one end of the court to the other. The key for Milan was to cover as much area as possible without becoming too spread out.

The Indians employed the half-court version of their zone press against Frankfort in the final quarter. Causing numerous turnovers, Milan scored 24 points in the last eight minutes—one more point than the 23 points with which they'd started the quarter. Unfortunately their comeback fell two points shy, but the use of the press in this game would later play a role in Milan's ultimate success. The Indians fell to Frankfort (49-47), but won the consolation game against Columbus (51-48).

The loss to Frankfort was a bitter one, but the tourney gave the Indians a critical shot of confidence. "I suppose we might have been a little 'gun shy' about playing those larger schools—especially after the whipping we'd taken against South Bend," Ray Craft explains. "I can't say it was as though we thought we'd lose or that we were not unhappy about that loss to Frankfort, but we did gain some confidence from playing in the tournament. We beat Columbus, a big school, and had a horrible shooting game against Frankfort. We left thinking that if we'd played to our potential then we could have won the tournament."

Bob Collins, a college friend of Marvin's and a sports reporter for the Indianapolis Star, saw Milan play in the Frankfort tourney. He came away from that game with a positive impression of the Indians. In fact, he devoted one of his columns to the team in which he suggested that Milan might even be good enough to win the state tournament. ". . . I'd seen Milan play in the state finals (in '53) . . . They were so far out of their league it was unbelievable," says Collins. "But in looking back I think that game with Central was a great learning experience [for Milan]. The next year I started writing a basketball column about the entire state. Although I'm a city boy I've always loved small-town basketball. Most of the basketball being written about in the Indianapolis papers was about Indianapolis schools, or schools from the North Central Conference, or the South Central Conference. Oh, there'd be a few stories from up in The Region or Terre Haute, but almost nothing about the small schools.

"I wanted to give the smaller schools a break, and, more than anything else, I wanted to see a small school win the state championship. Naturally, because of Woody, Milan was my first choice. I started to spend a lot time around them in '54. Of course, in those days it was unheard of for a so-called big city writer to write about a school like Milan. I even wrote that Milan was a contender for the state championship. People would come to me and tell me that I was absolutely crazy [to write such a thing]. When they lost up at that Frankfort Tourney they didn't get disgraced and after that I realized they had a good chance at winning the state tournament."

After the Frankfort tourney the Indians did not play another game until the County tournament. Their first-round opponent, Versailles, nearly beat the rusty Indians, but in the end Milan prevailed by six points. The close game with Versailles served as a wake-up call and the Indians swept past their next two opponents Napoleon (36-30) and Holton (44-30) to win their third straight County championship.

The Indians continued their winning ways with victories over Napoleon (61-29), Hanover (38-32), Sunman (42-30), Versailles (49-42), and North Vernon (38-37). It was during the Versailles contest that Marvin insisted his lads play man-to-man defense. They trailed through three quarters before pulling out the victory. They were not as fortunate against Aurora.

The game with Aurora was the next-to-the-last game of the season. By that time both Milan and Aurora had begun to raise a few eyebrows in Indianapolis and parts beyond. This recognition earned the Red Devils a #10 ranking in the high school polls with Milan not far behind at #14. The taller Red Devils led by talented Bob Fehrman soundly defeated Milan by a 54-45 score. The margin of defeat would have been larger if not for the "half-court zone trap" employed by Milan in the later stages of the ballgame.

Milan closed the season with a 38-30 victory over Osgood and entered the sectional as the solid favorites for the second consecutive year.

The 44th annual state basketball tournament began with Milan facing Cross Plains. Posting their twentieth victory of the season, the Indians jumped out to an 18-3 lead and never looked back. Four Indians scored in double figures as they walloped the Wildcats 83-36. In the semi-final game against Osgood, the Indians fashioned a similar start. Leading 27-13 at the half, they coasted to a 44-30 triumph. The championship contest featured arch-nemesis Versailles. This would be the fourth meeting between the two schools with Milan winning all three of the previous games. Milan pushed to a 28-18 lead, but saw the lead dwindle to two points (29-27) early in the third quarter. The Indians re-grouped and nursed that lead up to ten points before retiring to their "cat and mouse" tactics which took the "snarl" out of the Lions. Milan won 57-43. They'd beaten the Lions four times in one season and secured their second consecutive trip to Rushville.

The sectional championship had been expected and the Indians had achieved it with an efficiency bordering on perfection. The loss against Aurora had stung them and from that point they'd played like a well-oiled machine. "I thought we were playing pretty well," Marvin recalls. "But I knew a lot of things could happen in a state tournament. I hoped we hadn't peaked too early."

Milan's opponent in the afternoon game of the Rushville regional was the host school, Rushville. The Lions were no match for the Indians. The 58-34 final was a far cry from the double overtime victory and the ensuing clock controversy of the previous year. This victory set up a return match between Milan and Aurora, who'd trounced unruly Connersville.

The Red Devils posed a difficult obstacle in the road to Indianapolis. In Bob Fehrman and Ron Klingerhoffer they had two of the better big men in the state and with Jerry Drew at guard they also had an outside threat. In the afternoon contest Fehrman set a regional single-game scoring record with 35 points. The task of containing 6'5" Fehrman belonged to 5'11" Gene White. Given the structure of Milan's defense, White could expect help from Ron Truitt and Bob Engel.

Milan leaped to a 6-1 lead, but this advantage soon disappeared. The game settled down to a see-saw affair with the teams alternating the lead throughout the first and early stages of the second quarter. Then Jerry Drew caught fire and hit three straight long ones while Milan went cold. The Red Devils built a nine-point lead with 1:16 remaining in the half. Wood, sensing the game slipping out of control, had his team hold the ball for a final shot. Plump hit a jumper with time running out and the first half ended with Aurora out in front 27-20.

When play began in the third quarter, Aurora continued to hold a seven-point lead. Utilizing their big men to hold the Indians at bay, the Red Devils led 34-25. Then, with less than two minutes remaining in the canto, Marvin switched defenses to the zone press. The Indians worked the press to perfection causing Aurora to struggle just to get the ball past the ten second line. In the last two minutes of the third quarter the Red Devils twice violated the "ten-second rule" and committed three other turnovers. By the end of the quarter the Indians cut the Aurora lead to 34-28.

The fourth quarter brought more of the same and Aurora simply had no answer for the pressing defense. When Milan edged ahead 39-36, Indian fans expelled a collective sigh of relief—Milan had the lead and now they'd go into the "cat and mouse" to salt away the victory. Coach Wood, however, had other plans. He continued to let his two forwards, Truitt and Engel, bomb away from the outside. Such a tactic confused everyone, especially the Red Devils, who soon fell behind by 10 points. With a ten point lead and 1:12 left in the game, Marvin sent in his reserves who "stalled" for a 46-36 victory and the Indians second Regional title.

When fans arrived at Arkenberg's drugstore, which was the meeting place after Indian ball games, their discussions focused on this newest twist introduced by Coach Wood. "Of course, we'll never forget the first time he used the stall," remembers Betty Dobson, a Milan resident and Indian fan. "We always met at Arkenberg's after the ball game and when he first used that stall, well, the arguments for and against it ran pretty hot."

"Its kind of funny to look back at the Aurora game and remember how folks reacted to Marvin not using it," adds Betty's husband, Barter. "We'd grown used to the boys getting a lead and then sitting on it. When they didn't, some of us got a little nervous."

Gene White remembers trying in vain to get his teammates to go into the "cat and mouse. "Every once in a while I'd get the guys to go into that thing. And I tried that night, but Engel and Truitt kept putting them up and the shots kept going in and we got further and further ahead."

Bob Engel, who scored a team-leading seventeen points in the ball game recalls one of the town's leading citizens in complete disarray after that game. "A gentleman who lived in town, Duke Kohlmeyer, had stood beneath the basket while we were warming up. He liked to come down and talk to us. I'll never forget how he looked before that game. He was perfectly dressed; nice beige sport coat, pale green shirt, and a green tie. After the game I looked down beneath the basket on the far end of the court and there was Duke Kohlmeyer. He had his sport coat hanging over his arm, his tie off, his shirt tail out, and his shirt unbuttoned. I'm tellin' you, it looked like he'd been in a fight. His hair was disarrayed and that man could not talk until the next day. When he did talk the first thing he asked me was 'Why the hell didn't you go into the control (cat and mouse)?' He said, 'You guys made me mad.' He'd hollered so much at me and Truitt that he lost his voice. He was screaming at us to go into the control, but Truitt and I were tearin' the nets off that night..."

"We normally would use the cat and mouse in that situation," Wood explains. "But we didn't that night because of what I was reading on the faces of those Aurora kids. Our press had taken the life out of them and it was one of those situations where we had a couple of guys with 'hot hands' and Aurora wasn't hurting us when they had the ball. They could not attack the press and their turnovers were giving us easy shots at the basket."

The pressing Indians held Aurora to only nine points in the entire second half—and of those nine only two came in the fourth quarter. Milan, on the other hand, scored eighteen points in the final quarter and most came as the result of Aurora turnovers. Gene White's defense on Bob Fehrman held the Red Devils scoring ace to twelve points while no other Red Devil scored in double figures. Engel and Plump paced the Milan attack and Ron Truitt's timely buckets helped to demoralize the confused Red Devil defense.

In avenging their regular season loss to Aurora, the Indians earned a return trip to the Indianapolis Semi-Final, where they would face Montezuma (23-5). The match-up was unique in the fact that Montezuma, too, was a small community. A school with only 40 boys, the Aztecs featured a 5″0″ guard, Bill Knoblett. The remaining Aztecs had height. Their forwards Ronnie Baumann and Dick Pitman were especially talented.

In the Milan-Montezuma contest the Indians got off to a great start, leading 20-10 at the end of the first quarter and 29-21 at the half. Then, scoring only three points, Milan struggled through the third period while the Aztecs got back in the ball game. With the score tied at thirty and time running out in the quarter, Plump hit a bucket to give the Indians a slim 32-30 lead.

The Aztecs pushed ahead by six in the fourth but Milan struggled to within two with less than five minutes remaining. "As I look back, it occurs to me that we always struggled against the smaller schools," Marvin recalls. "Morton Memorial and Attica gave us fits in '53—and Montezuma had us in deep trouble in '54. We had to fight like heck to get back in that ball game. At one point I remember thinking that we'd gotten this far and now we were going to get beat by the only team in the tournament smaller than us." But Milan, stung to life by the Aztec's spirited play, scored the game's last twelve points to win 44-34. "The boys passed a 'gut test' in those last four minutes," says Marvin. "They played with the most intensity I'd seen all season."

As they had in '53, Milan played the first game of the afternoon. The second contest pitted Crispus Attucks against a plucky Columbus ball club, which the Indians had earlier beaten by a 51-48 margin. Marvin and his players hoped Columbus would upset Attucks because they felt they had a pretty good chance at beating the Bulldogs again. As the team ate lunch at the Apex Grill on 16th street they listened to the ball game. Columbus broke out to a 10 point lead, but the Tigers, led by Bill Mason and Oscar Robertson, slowly chewed at the Bulldog's lead. And, in a thrilling ending, came up the victors by a 68-67 score.

The second contest pitted Crispus Attucks against a plucky Columbus ball club, which the Indians had earlier beaten by a 51-48 margin. Marvin and his players hoped Columbus would upset Attucks because they felt they had a pretty good chance at beating the Bulldogs again. As the team ate lunch at the Apex Grill on 16th street they listened to the ball game. Columbus broke out to a 10 point lead, but the Tigers, led by Bill Mason and Oscar Robertson, slowly chewed at the Bulldog's lead. And, in a thrilling ending, came up the victors by a 68-67 score.

The evening's finale featured Milan and Attucks. Despite the Tigers reputation and #1 ranking, the Indians were certain they could compete. "After Attucks made that great comeback to win, Roger Schroeder got up from the table and said: 'Well, it looks like we're gonna have to beat Attucks,'" Gene White recalls. "He said 'beat Attucks,' 'not play Attucks,' and that pretty much summed up the way we felt about it. We preferred to play Columbus because we knew them, but if it was Attucks well then, bring them on."

The Milan-Attucks Semi-Final championship was marred by racist undertones as the white community of Indianapolis did not support the hometown team, but rather hurled racists remarks at them throughout the contest. "I guess the first time the race issue really hit home was when the proprietor there at the Apex asked us what we thought about having to play the black boys," Bob Engel recalls. "I don't think there was one of us who knew how to answer. We were a lot more concerned about the quality of basketball we'd heard they could play than we were about the color of their skin."

"Yes, in retrospect I'd have to say it was absolutely terrible," Bobby Plump adds. "I don't think it ever really dawned on us what all of that was about. We were naive farm kids who didn't know much at all about that kind of thing. But as I look back I think that was most unfortunate. The guys from Attucks, Crenshaw, Mason, Robertson, Mitchell, and their coach Ray Crowe were probably the finest sportsmen we played that year. They were tough competitors and good sports. Considering the treatment they received from the crowd, I think they were an amazing team."

The two teams played a clean, highly entertaining contest. The Indians got out to a 6-0 lead, but Oscar Robertson got Attucks back in the game with his team's first 5 points. Trailing 13-9 with 3:27 remaining in the first, Attucks slowly bent the Indians to their will and at the :27 mark took their first lead 17-16. The lead changed hands several times during the opening minutes of the second quarter. By the half, however, Milan had edged its way to a 39-32 advantage. The Indians gained that seven point advantage by running a patient offense and dominating the boards. Without the consistent scoring of sophomore sensation Oscar Robertson the Milan lead could have easily been over ten points.

"If I had not been so concerned about what he was doing to our defense, watching Oscar Robertson would have been a treat," Wood recalls. "He was still young and wasn't quite as tall as he got to be a few years later, but he was already an extremely talented ballplayer. He had a great game against us."

Milan started the second half with a quick basket from Truitt before slowing things down. Leading by eleven mid-way through the third period, the Indians went into a dribbling stall with Plump and Craft sharing the ball handling duties. For two full minutes they played keep away. The quarter ended with another Robertson long shot, but the Indians held a 49-39 advantage.

Milan used their "cat and mouse" in the fourth causing the frustrated Tigers to foul and hope the Indians missed their freethrows. The Indians hit their freethrows and went on to a 65-52 victory. Bobby Plump tallied 28 points for the victors while Oscar Robertson had 22 for Attucks.

Marvin thinks his team played their best game against Attucks. The win was especially rewarding because it came as a result of staying with the fundamentals he'd preached all year long. "Clarence Kelly did most of our scouting and when he read the report on Attucks I got cold chills," Marvin recalls. "They were big and quick and Ray Crowe was an excellent

Mary Lou gives Marvin a hug after 1954 Semi-final victory.

coach and strategist. But Kelly always ended his summations with suggestions as to what might work against each opponent. He pointed out a few weaknesses in Attucks that I thought we might be able to exploit.I thought our press could give them trouble and our Hinkle offense would get us good shots.

"We started the game with some easy baskets and were surprised at the trouble the 'Hinkle' gave them. Our zone press worked well and we could beat their press by quickly in-bounding the ball and then throwing it down the sidelines. This was simply an extension of our fastbreak, which was something we practiced every day. We did not do anything special to beat them, but I will say that each of our guys had one of the best games of their high school career. We played our kind of game and we played it well."

This story is told of an incident that occurred during Marvin's playing days at Butler. "The Bulldogs one night went tearing down the floor, laid in a basket and ambled back chatting among themselves about how well they'd done that. But— whoosh—the other team came racing back and also scored. Woody immediately turned to his teammates and yelled: 'Hey you guys let's not be talking over our glory so long.' In this respect, Marvin the coach was not much different than Marvin the player. Each victory in the Indians second trip through the state tournament gave them plenty to crow about. Instead they followed the example set by their coach—they got back to work on improving their play.

As the 1953-54 season wound down to its final week, the media found it impossible not to delve deeper into the story of little Milan. In examining this community they found these lads were not much different than small-town boys from around the state—and yet there were those subtle things that made all the difference in the world.

One such difference was the "open air stadium," a basketball court of gravel and cinders with a hoop hung precariously close to a manure pile ("If you lost your balance you could fall into that stuff clear up to your shoulders," Whitey once confessed). It was on this court that Plump and White and some of the others practiced and practiced and practiced. They loved the game of basketball and by playing as much as they did they'd become some of the better players in the state.

These, too, were smart kids. They did their thinking in the classroom as well as on the basketball court. The town was blessed with excellent teachers in the school system. An example of this excellence could be found in the high school principal, Cale Hudson. Realizing that most of the boys might have the chance to go to college, Hudson added a math course to help with their preparation. "I remember Mr. Hudson did some great counseling with some of us one day in the library," Gene White recalls, "Truitt, Schroeder, Craft, and I were just lounging around. It was our senior year we all had enough credits to graduate and we had several study halls—we thought we had it made. Then Mr. Hudson walked in and said: 'Boys I'm starting a class in solid geometry and you and you and you are in it.' That's what I call good counseling."

Perhaps the most important element in Milan's success was the brains and determination of Marvin Wood. Marvin had matured since his first coaching assignment at French Lick. He could look back at his college experience and remember the words of his mentor, Tony Hinkle. Hinkle had said Marvin would be a good coach, but he had some things to learn that he'd pick up along the way. Hinkle was right. Marvin did have some lessons to learn. He learned them well and at age twenty-six he'd already become a teacher. Among his pupils was his old coach, Tony Hinkle, who copied Marvin's "cat and mouse" offense as did the coach at Michigan State. No more than four years out of college, Marvin had become one of the most innovative basketball coaches in the land. And now, for the second season in a row, he'd take his team back into Indianapolis for a shot at the state title.

During the weeks of the tournament, the town of Milan buzzed with excitement. Gene White's mother, Genevieve, fondly recalls those days. "Gene's father and I operated a feed store," Mrs. White recalls, "Milan was mostly a farming community so the feed store was a meeting place for a lot of the farmers. During those weeks of the tournament, we had a steady stream of people in our store, but I don't think many of them bought much—they just came to talk about the basketball team.

"It's kinda funny because when Milan had made it to the regional back in '46 Gene's father and I decided that we just had to take little Gene to see the regional up in Rushville. We figured that it would be a long time before the school would get that far in the tournament again and we wanted our son to have a chance to see a regional."

The success of the team had a strange effect on the local economy. Egg-laying chickens, for example, were cheap because of a glut on the market. Folks who'd been following the team did not have the time to tend to them. The same was true of milk cows. In Fountaintown Marvin's father and uncle were forced to put extra trucks on the milk routes so they could complete their work in time to watch Milan's games.

Perhaps the most difficult situation brought on by the Indian's success was that confronted by Cale Hudson who had the responsibility of distributing tickets. "... I think the first notion I got as to how difficult it would be to be the ticket manager at Milan came during my interview for the principal's job," Cale recalls. "The board asked me some questions as to how I might handle different situations regarding the distribution of tickets. Apparently, my predecessor had problems during the 52-53 season, and, in fact, he disappeared during April and they never heard from him again.

"It was difficult to please everyone, but we tried our best to be fair. For example, during the state final in '54 we had 950 be fair. For example, during the state final in '54 we had 950 tickets to distribute. From that number I had to set aside tickets for the coaches and their families, the team and their families, the faculty, and a few others. To distribute the rest we decided to have everybody in the school district who wanted tickets to sign up for them. We knew that we would not have enough tickets for everyone. We also knew that some people would sign up for those tickets and then they'd go out and scalp them. So, we decided to have a public drawing. We held the drawing in such a way that those people whose names were drawn came forward and payed for their tickets. We gave them a receipt and told them they could pick up their tickets from me at the door of the fieldhouse on the day of the game. We hoped this would eliminate having those tickets out there to be traded around ... Of course, I held my breath because I'd been killed if someone got up there and didn't get a ticket, but that part of it worked out.

"After people first signed up we decided to have a County trustee look over the list. He identified people who'd been dead for five years. A guy signed his grandmother up who'd been in a nursing home for a couple of years and so on. Anyway, the trustee helped us eliminate quite a few names from the list. In the end I think we did a pretty good job of getting the tickets into the hands of the people who wanted them."

While Cale struggled with the duties of a ticket manager, the dinner crowd at Arkenberg's or at the Railroad Inn speculated as to what strategies coach Wood might employ to help the Indian's secure two more victories—it is safe to say that not a one of them even came close to guessing what would happen...

1954 Final Four Coaches meet with Commissioner L. V. Phillips left to right: Marvin Wood-Milan, Bill Milner-Elkhart, Commissioner Phillips, Howard Sharpe-Terre Haute Gerstmeyer, Jay McCreary-Muncie. (Courtesy Indianapolis Star)

Left to right: Ron Truitt, Ken Wendleman, Ray Craft, Roger Schroder and Gene White talk to Bobby Plump in car. (Courtesy Indianapolis Star)

Terre Haute Gerstmeyer, the Indians afternoon opponent, came into the contest ranked #2 in the state. They featured a high powered offense anchored by Arley and Uncle Harold Andrews. Gerstmeyer had been runner-up in the '53 tournament and was a favorite of many to capture the title. The Terre Haute-Milan match-up followed the Muncie Central-Elkhart game, which was won in convincing fashion by the the Muncie Central Bearcats 59-50.

"We felt like we got a big plus by having to face Terre Haute," Marvin explains. "Muncie and Elkhart were big, physical ball clubs. We thought if we could get by Gerstmeyer, then the evening match-up would be a little easier because the two physical teams would beat each other up in the afternoon game.

"I had an excellent scouting report on Gerstmeyer. Gerl Furr scouted them for me. When he told me that they planned to attack our zone by putting their best shooter in the middle, I couldn't believe it. By doing that they would be playing into our hands. So, going into that game I figured we'd have a good chance at completely shutting off one of their best shooters."

Another factor looming large in Marvin's mind was the condition of his star forward, Bob Engel. Engel had suffered from a lower back problem during most of the tournament. Against Attucks he further damaged it and would be playing with a great deal of pain. Marvin did not know how many minutes he would get from Engel.

The game began with Gerstmeyer scoring the first four points. Then Milan came roaring back. The Indians scored twenty one points in seven minutes to lead 21-12 at the quarter break. Terre Haute made several attempts to get back into the game but, with Arley Andrews playing in the middle of Milan's stingy zone, the Black Cats were unable to get the ball into the hands of one of their better shooters. On Milan's end the "cat and mouse" shredded the Gerstmeyer defense, giving Milan numerous opportunities to score. With time running out in the first half Terre Haute rallied to pull within two, but in the last minute Plump had two steals and two buckets bumping the Milan lead to six at the half.

Plump and Milan continued to dominate the Gerstmeyer defense in the second half. Scoring almost at will and harassing the offense on the other end, the Indians stayed out of trouble and coasted to a shocking 60-48 victory. The Milan defense held

Arley Andrews to 2 of 11 from the field and Plump led all scorers with twenty-eight points.

"We knew they were weak on individual defense," Marvin explains. "They played great defense as a team, but when we got them spread out with the cat and mouse they could not contain us."

Defensively, Marvin had his assistant coach, Clarence Kelly, spend time working with Gene White on screening out and staying between his man and the basket. "I worked very hard with Gene," Clarence recalls, 'Pin him, hook him, hang on to his shirt, pull on his pants. Do anything you can to disrupt him . . . So what if he weighs 225. Get around him. Get him out of the way.' These were the things I told him day after day. Come game day—that's exactly what ole' Whitey did."

On Milan's end of the court Terre Haute failed to defense Milan's varied offenses and they could not stop Bobby Plump. "Plump just killed them," White laughs. "They absolutely could not deal with him. I'll never forget one play where he came down the middle of the floor on a fastbreak and gave his defender a head-and-shoulders fake. It sat that kid right on his butt. I've never seen that before or since."

Having upset the Black Cats, Milan helped create one of the most intriguing championship games in the tournament's history. Muncie Central, a perennial contender for the title, was in pursuit of an unprecedented fifth state basketball title. The Bearcats, coached by Jay McCreary, were a powerful ball club. They featured a rugged front line, anchored by 6'5" John Casterlow, 6'4" Jimmy Hinds, and 6'2" Gene Flowers. Guards Jimmy Barnes and Phil Raisor rounded out the Muncie starting five which achieved it objectives through the use of brute force. Milan, on the other hand, hoped to achieve a storybook ending to a dream season. No small school had won the state championship since 1915. The Indians had no players over 6'2". They hoped their quickness and experience would enable them to overcome the disparity in height.

In this "David versus Goliath" match-up, the crowd favored David. Muncie Central cheerleaders and a thin line of purple-clad fans which ran from the first row of seats on up to the rafters were the only signs of Bearcat support. Muncie might have been the larger school and community, but as the arena filled for the final game it became apparent that more than just the Milan faithful had come to root for an Indian victory.

As the teams ran from the tunnel onto the floor, the crowd broke into a roar which would ebb and flow throughout the contest. "I can honestly say I wasn't nervous," Gene White smiles as he remembers the opening moments of that game. "If I were to be real honest I'd have to say that I was thinking that we'd already won that silver ring which was more than we'd done the last time. Now, I don't think that affected my play, but I'm sure that someone in the crowd might have said: Whitey's playing like he's content with that silver ring."

The Indians controlled the opening tip but lost possession without taking a shot. Muncie quickly took advantage of the Indian error as Gene Flowers got the game's first two points with a bucket from the outside. Milan continued to have problems finding the handle on the ball and when Bobby Plump fouled Jimmy Barnes the Bearcat hit the freethrow and gave Muncie a 3-0 lead.

Ray Craft, fouled in the act of shooting, got Milan's first two points on a pair of freethrows. Muncie responded with a bucket from Jimmy Hinds but Craft again countered for Milan making the score 5-4.

The Bearcats had made it known they intended to make life miserable for Milan's ace shooter, Bobby Plump, which was exactly what they did with their next possession. As Plump tried to guard against an easy bucket on a Muncie fastbreak, the Bearcat's 6'4" Jimmy Hinds crashed into Plump,and sent him sprawling across the slick wooden floor. The ref whistled an offensive foul and a woozy Plump hit the the freebie to tie the game at five.

Seconds later, ailing Bob Engel hit a beautiful twenty-five foot two-handed set shot to give Milan their first lead. Ronnie Truitt fouled Hinds in the act of shooting and the Muncie lad hit both freethrows to tie it back up with 4:17 left in the first. Muncie then went back into the lead when Jimmy Barnes nailed a long one from the corner. During Milan's next possesion John Casterlow fouled Gene White who hit the freethrow cutting the Muncie lead to 9-8.

Bobby Plump hit layup at 2:40. Jimmy Barnes then countered with a basket for Muncie. Trailing 11-10 the Indians went on the warpath and scored four points to close the quarter with a 14-11 lead.

In the huddle between quarters, the Indians now knew that they could play ball with their larger opponents. Marvin smiles as he relates a little of what went on in between-quarter pow-wow. "Gene White said to me, 'I can push him, I can pull him, I can take him anywhere you want me to.' He was referring to 6'5" John Casterlow who had six inches and fifty pounds on Whitey, but playing those first eight minutes gave him and the team confidence that they could indeed win the ball game."

Early in the second quarter, Milan pushed its lead to six points. Leading 17-11 behind a Craft freethrow and a Truitt jump hook, the Indians slowed their pace and began looking for layups. At 5:56 Ray Craft found one and gave the Indians a 19-11 advantage. Muncie took a timeout.

When the claxon brought both teams back onto the court the Bearcats re-grouped behind another Hind's jumper from the outside. Ray Craft was fouled and hit the freebie. Gene Flowers hit a corner shot for the Bearcats. The Indians then answered with three of their own. Leading 23-15, Milan was content to take their time on offense. Muncie, on the other hand, pushed the ball upcourt as fast as they could. On their end the Bearcat's height and brawn earned them numerous rebounds one of which they converted into two points, cutting the Milan lead to 23-17 at the half.

As the teams disappeared into the dressing rooms for a brief respite, deep in the heart of Texas, Marvin's brother, Wayne, sat in his parked car on a hill near the army base where he was stationed. From the top of the hill his car radio caught the faint signal of Ft. Wayne's WOWO. He and his wife listened to the game with their hearts in their throats. In Florida vacationing Hoosiers found "hot spots" along certain streets where they could catch the game on their car radios. One story is told of a Vero Beach policeman who'd been called to investigate "a strange gathering of people" along one of the city streets. These basketball fans explained, and the policeman thrice came back to check on the score.

Back in the fieldhouse the cheers of 15,000 fans settled to a din. While the players took a rest, the spectators sipped a beverage and finally sat in the seats for which they'd paid, but had yet to use. Muncie fans were nervous but felt confident that their boys would erase the Milan lead and capture their fifth title. Milan's six-point lead tantilized the rest of the spectators with the possibility of a fairy-tale ending.

In the Bearcat locker room Coach McCreary stressed hitting the boards and blocking the passing lanes. On the Milan side

Marvin learned that Bob Engel was through for the night. He exhorted his players to look for the fastbreak, but to be patient if it wasn't there. He wanted them to communicate with each other on defense and to block out.

Muncie Central opened the second half with four straight points, causing Marvin to call a timeout. Marvin told his boys to continue to use the "cat and mouse" and to be more aggressive in their zone. Back out on the floor Plump tried a drive to the basket and was fouled. He hit the freebie, but Muncie countered with one of two free ones from Gene Flowers, who'd been hacked by Gene White. Truitt got another free one for Milan. Muncie then cut the lead to one with a basket by Hinds.

With the score 25-24 in favor of Milan, officials stopped play to clear the floor of ice thrown by an over-exuberant fan. This pause came with 4:51 left in the third. "Right around that time, I felt the game was slipping from our grasp," Marvin admits. "Despite the fact we'd been able to out score them, we'd been taking a beating all game long. Plump had been run over in the first of the game and he was not the same after that. I could see we were wearing down. We'd had to do a lot of jumping for rebounds and we weren't getting many of them—I think that wore us down both mentally and physically . . .

"Leading 19-11 we'd gone into our ball control to help eliminate some of the physical play—this was bad for us because they got the opportunity to make some adjustments at halftime. When they came out in the second half they were much better prepared to defend against the ball control and they were much more aggressive."

Marvin hoped his team could hang on, but began to ponder over changes he might make to shift the momentum back to Milan. Returning to play, the Indians patiently moved the ball, looking for a good shot. But the Muncie defense continued to frustrate them. Finally, Ray Craft found dribbling room and made a dash to the basket, only to be fouled by Leon Agullana before he could shoot. Craft hit the charity toss, but the Bearcats roared down to their end, put up and rebounded three shots, and finally scored on a Agullana one-hander. The basket tied the game, but Agullana fouled Ray Craft in the process.

In 1954 common fouls drew one freethrow. However, if the freethrow shooter missed his first attempt, he was awarded with a second try. With 1:20 left in the third, Ray Craft, the Indian's best scorer of the night missed both freethrows. The quarter ended in a 26-26 tie. In the first eight minutes of the second half Muncie's defense had limited Milan to zero field goals in seven attempts.

The Indians found themselves in a heap of trouble. Muncie had dictated the tempo in the third quarter and thus had gained momentum. Marvin knew his team could not win unless they dictated the pace of the game. At the beginning of the fourth quarter he took drastic action to reverse the momentum.

Muncie garnered the fourth quarter tip and, when Ronnie Truitt fouled Jim Hinds who converted two freethrows, the Bearcats had their first lead since early in the first quarter. Trailing 26-28, Milan slowly brought the ball down to their end of the court and ran their ball control offense. The Bearcats were prepared for this and sagged back in around the basket to prevent the easy shot Milan coveted. The Indians worked their weave for about a minute and then Plump retired to beyond the top of the circle where he tucked the ball under his arm and waited.

The Bearcats, leading by two, were content with this arrangement and continued to linger below the circle . . . And Plump continued to hold the ball. After a minute or so, the roar of the crowd became so loud that it was impossible to converse in a normal tone of voice. Barter Dobson, a Milan resident and driver for the team, remembers the noise and excitement. ". . . It was unreal. My wife was so nervous that she had to keep her head down for fear of throwing up . . . People were fainting and those of us cheering for Milan were especially nervous. We had no idea what Coach Wood intended to do. Afterall, we were losing and we couldn't figure out why he'd want to stall when we were behind." Two minutes passed and Plump continued to hold the ball.

"We were surprised that Muncie let us do this," Marvin recalls. "They had the speed and size and yet here they were letting us dictate the tempo. The longer they let us stand, the more time we had to set up a strategy for the remaining minutes of the ball game—which is exactly what we did. I decided we'd bring the clock down to about three minutes and then change both our offense and defense. On offense we were going to go back to the Hinkle system and hope that they would not adjust to it. This would give us a chance at a few easy backets. On defense we planned to use the half-court zone trap. It had worked well on several occasions when we were behind—most notably against my friend, Marvin Cave, in the Frankfort Holiday Tourney. Earlier in the week Cave mentioned to me that he'd used the press against Muncie. He said it gave them fits." (In fact, Marvin Cave was the only spectator in the building to hold the distinction of having coached a team that had beaten both Milan and Muncie Central.)

Plump continued to hold the ball until the clock spun down to 3:00. Then he called timeout. "To give you an idea of the kind of chemistry we had at Milan," Marvin explains. "When the boys came over they already knew we were going to change our defense to the press, but they didn't know that we would change our offense."

Having made these adjustments, the Indians started moving the ball. At 2:45 Plump found a lane to the hoop, but missed the shot. Muncie cornered the rebound but Milan's press surprised the Bearcats causing them to make a turnover. Ray Craft's jumper at 2:14 tied the game at 28. On Muncie's end the Bearcats could not solve the trapping press. Hinds took an ill-advised shot from the corner which careened off the rim and into Gene White's hands. The Indians quickly moved the ball to Bobby Plump, who was immediately fouled by Jimmy Barnes.

Back in '54 any foul committed with less than two minutes left in the game resulted in two shots. Barnes' foul came with 1:38 left and Plump hit both freethrows to give Milan a 30-28 lead. The zone press then caused another bad pass from Barnes, which the Indians recovered. Leading by two and back in their "cat and mouse," Milan worked diligently for the best available shot. Craft found one but his layup rolled twice around the rim and fell out giving Muncie a chance to get back in the game.

The Bearcats solved the Milan press with a long pass to Gene Flowers beneath the basket. He hit the layup to tie the game at 30 with :48 left. The Indians worked the ball down court, stalling until :18 when they called a timeout. "I decided we were going to take one more shot and Bobby Plump was going to be the one to take it," Marvin explains. "We'd set up a play where Craft would throw the ball into Plump who'd work it until the clock got down to eight or nine seconds. From there I told him to get the best shot available. I told the other four players to stay out of the way. Gene White suggested that they all line up out in the perimeter along the left side of the circle. I thought it was an excellent suggestion and that is exactly what they did."

By the time Milan and Muncie came back on the court the crowd was in a frenzy. Amid the deafening din the Indians started their final play by making a mistake. "Ray was supposed to throw the ball into me, but for some reason I ended up throwing it into him," Plump explains, describing those final eighteen seconds. "In retrospect it was probably better that we screwed it up because by me throwing the ball into Ray and then getting it back from him—it allowed me to not give up my dribble . . . When I crossed the center line, Barnes wasn't guarding me too closely. I think he was afraid that I might drive around him. I made a few head fakes and I remember looking at the clock and thinking that I'd have to wait just a few more seconds to make my move. I'd been having a terrible game and hoped things would work out so I'd get an opportunity to redeem myself.

". . . When I started my drive Barnes dropped way off of me and I remember being surprised because everything was open. He wasn't going to give me a layup, but I knew I could get a decent shot from 12-15 feet . . . I've always said a shooter knows when a shot is going in—when that ball left my hands I knew it was good."

Plump's shot sagged through the net, igniting an explosion from the crowd, which all but buried the sound of the final horn sealing Milan's 32-30 victory.

1954 State Final afternoon game Milan versus Terre Haute Gerstmeyer: Uncle Harold Andrews blocks Ray Craft's layup while Ken Wendleman and Rollin Cutter look on. (Courtesy Indianapolis Star)

Bobby Plump fights Jack Smith for the ball. (Courtesy Indianapolis Star)

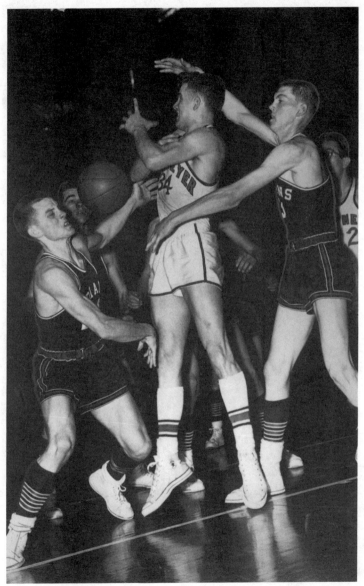

*Ron Truitt (RT) and Ray Craft battle Arley Andrews for a rebound.
(Courtesy Indianapolis Star)*

Ray Craft and Gene White chase a loose ball. (Courtesy Indianapolis Star)

Bobby Plump hits the floor for a loose ball against Bill Bolk while Bob Engel (5) and Jack Smith look on. (Courtesy Indianapolis Star)

*1954 State Final Championship game Milan versus Muncie Central.
Cheering at Final Game - center Mary Lou Wood and her sister
Veralee (Henley) Lain.*

Jimmy Hinds floors bobby Plump early in the game. Jim Barnes, Ron Truitt, Bob Engel, and John Casterlow are in the background. (Courtesy Indianapolis Star)

Jimmy Hinds fouls Ray Craft as he heads to the hoop. (Courtesy Indianapolis Star)

Bobby Plump (5'10") attempts a lay-up against Jim Hinds (6'4") and Robert Crawford (6'4"). (Courtesy Indianapolis Star)

Marvin Tood whistles a foul against Leon Agullana (21). Ray Craft is the victim. (Courtesy Indianapolis Star)

Ray Craft's lay-up late in the game rolled in and out. (Courtesy Indianapolis Star)

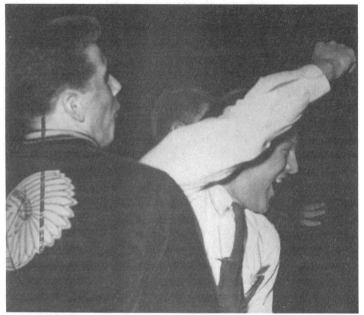

Coach Wood and Bill Jordan react to Bobby's "last shot". (Courtesy Indianapolis Star)

A dejected Muncie Central reacts to Plump's "last shot". (from left to right-sitting: Jimmy Barnes, Phil Raisor, Leon Agullana, John Casterlow, Gene Flowers; from left to right-standing: Principal Loren Chastain, Asst. Coach Carl Adams, a school official and Jim Hinds) (Courtesy Indianapolis Star)

The scoreboard tells the story . . .

Marvin gets a victory ride from Ron Truitt and Bobby Plump as the team looks on.

Gene White hugs cheerleader Patty Bohlke. (Courtesy Indianapolis Star)

"Cutting the net" - Mary Lou
Wood as Marvin holds the ladder.

Sid Collins interviews Coach
Wood.

Marvin snips the net.

1954 Milan state champs: Mascot David Jordan in front. Front row left to right: Principal Cale Hudson, Gene White, Ron Truitt, Bobby Plump, Ray Craft, Coach Wood. Row 2 left to right: Asst. Coach Clarence Kelly, Roger Schroder, Bob Engel, Glen Butte, Bill Jordan, Rollin Cutter, Manager Fred Busching, Ken Wendleman, Manager Oliver Jones and Asst. Coach Mark Combs.

March 22, 1954 Celebration Mary Lou Wood: "It's nice to be important, but it's more important to be nice."

Bob Collins addresses the crowd.

Ken Wendleman and Ray Craft present the State Championship Trophy to the community.

Cheerleaders Marjorie Ent, Virginia Voss and Patty Bohlke lead the crowd in a cheer while the team looks on.

Forty thousand fans celebrate the "mighty men of Milan" as they return home. (All Photos Courtesy Indianapolis News)

7

After "The Shot"

The aftermath of the exciting contest brought a collage of emotions and memorable moments. An entire state had sat on the edge of its seat for thirty-two minutes of emotion-charged basketball. At the game's conclusion it heaved a collective sigh. Those who'd rooted for Muncie shed tears of sorrow and those who were for Milan wore huge smiles on their tear-stained cheeks. As Corky Lamm of the Indianapolis News wrote: "It started out as a fairy tale and ended an epic. This was Indiana's 44th high school basketball tournament, with a championship game so dramatic, so unbelievable, so delicious you think that maybe for the first time the old-fashioned superlatives won't do. . ."

"When Plump hit that bucket I heard this tremendous roar behind me," Marvin recalls. "The sound just rolled over us. Then one of the kids on the bench next to me put his arms around my neck and was screaming 'We won! We won!' It was one of the most special moments of my life."

As tournament officials tried to get the crowd back into their seats for the awards ceremony, Marvin and his team stared at each other in amazement over what had happened. "They were trying to get everybody calmed down to do the award ceremony and it still hadn't dawned on us exactly what had happened," Ray Craft explains. "We knew we'd won, but as quickly as it had happened and all, well, I think we were dazed for a moment."

Marvin was quick to share the glory with some of the people who helped him along the way. One such person was his high school coach and good friend, Gerl Furr. With tears in his eyes an aging Coach Furr recalls that special moment. "Marvin sought me out and as we hugged he said to me: 'Coach its really not fair. With all the knowledge you have and all of the good teams you've coached this should have happened to you.'"

Mary Lou also recalls how Marvin shared that special moment with her. "During the semi-state the papers ran a picture of me hugging Marvin in the middle of the court after the Attucks game. I don't remember what the caption said, but Marvin was telling me to get back on the sidelines. Later I was relating this to Gerl Furr, who'd seen the picture in the paper, and he told us that Howard Sharpe had let his wife help cut down the nets. Later that night after Gerl had left Marvin told me he'd let me help cut down the nets if we won next week.

"After the game I was excited and everyone kept asking me if I was going to go out on the court. I told them no because I'd gotten in trouble for doing that during the semi-final. I wanted to see if Marvin would keep his promise—he did. He sent Bob Plump in the stands to get me. I told Bobby what a great basket he'd made. He said, 'Yea, but it was the about the only one I made all night.' I think I responded by assuring him it was the right one to hit. I told him how proud and happy we all were. He asked me to come on out and help the team cut the nets. Imagine that, the game's hero coming up into the stands to escort me out onto the court! The next day some of the papers ran a picture of me on the ladder cutting the nets—I can't imagine anyone ever being more thrilled than we were that night."

The evening, which had transpired in a fashion here before only seen in moving pictures, had one more surprise in store for Marvin, Milan, and the state of Indiana. After the award ceremony for the runners-up and champions, fans waited in their seats for the announcement of the Trester Award winner, which is annually awarded to the final-four player who best exemplifies the sportsmanship associated with basketball in the state of Indiana. The fieldhouse fell silent and as the announcement was about to be made a voice from up near the rafters boomed out, "Give it to Plump!" Give it to Plump was what the commissioners did—marking the first time in the history of the tournament that the Trester Award went to a player on the winning team.

"To have one of my boys win that award made me proud," Marvin recalls. "We spent a lot of time emphasizing the importance of good sportsmanship and I'd always been impressed with the way Bobby handled himself." Plump, who by his own admission was shy and somewhat backward, handled the notoriety that went with winning such an award with grace and poise.

"I think that's been on of the greatest experiences I've had in coaching," Marvin explains. "The opportunity to see young men and women grow from the time they are freshmen in high school until the time they are seniors. Some of the changes you see in young people are unbelievable. Bobby is an exceptional example of that. Here was a lad who was painfully shy, yet, by the time he entered college he'd spoken to numerous groups of people and did it with poise and confidence."

As the emotionally-spent crowd filtered out of the fieldhouse, the Indians returned to their dressing room to change and celebrate their remarkable achievement. With the sportswriters crowding around him, straining to hear his every word, Marvin praised his assistant coaches and pointed to the outstanding performances by Ray Craft and Rollin Cutter, who had subbed for the ailing Bob Engel.

Chief among the questions asked by the sportswriters was the rationale behind Marvin's move to hold the ball while trailing. If such a move had backfired Wood would have become the biggest "goat" in the tourney's history. When the pundits pressed him about this decision Wood grinned and replied, "While the boys were holding the ball I was trying to think of something to do."

Across the hall beneath the fieldhouse, the vanquished Bearcats quietly waited to congratulate their conquerors from Milan. Coach McCreary did his best to console his players, but little could be said or done to remove the pain of losing such a close and important game.

"We had a proud ballclub," McCreary recalls. "In those days playing basketball for Muncie Central was not an easy thing to do. We had many talented ballplayers who did not even make the team. Those who did play, played with the understanding that with hard work they could go far in the tournament. The '54 ballclub was a proud, hardworking bunch of kids and believe me they took that loss hard.

"I remember John Casterlow, our senior center and one of the hardest workers in the bunch, sat in the corner with tears coursing down his face and he just sat there and sat there. Finally, when the other boys were showered and ready to go, I approached him and said, 'Come on John let's get dressed and head on back to Muncie town.' He looked up at me and I'll never forget what he said. He said, 'Coach, if you don't mind,

I'd like to sit here for just a few more minutes. This is the last time I'll ever wear this jersey and just want to make sure that I'll never forget what it was like.' I think that comment best sums up how our boys felt about putting on their uniform and representing their school."

McCreary, who'd won a state title in '52, had a great deal of respect for Marvin and the strategy he used. "Some people have said we were tired from playing Elkhart or we didn't scout Milan well enough. But I don't think that's true. We came out of the afternoon contest with Elkhart in great shape. Our boys had played two games a day for the last three weeks and we ran an awful lot to stay in shape. In addition to having played the first game in the afternoon, we got a chance to rest and watch Milan play Gerstmeyer. It might be true that we didn't do a lot of advance scouting on Milan, but I knew darn well what they'd be doing. The fact is, I'd seen the Hinkle system as a player at Indiana University and I'd coached against Tony Hinkle when Marvin was a player. I knew Marvin ran the Hinkle System. So, it wasn't necessary to worry about what they might do. I was more concerned about our boys executing on defense.

"... They were almost as big and quick as we were but I didn't think they could run with us," continues McCreary. "Marvin was smart enough to see this and he did the only thing he could do, which was hold the ball. I don't understand why he waited until they got behind to do it ... When they took timeout with little time left, we felt we had a chance to win. My instruction to our players was to line up at an angle between their man and the basket. We knew they'd give the ball to Plump and we knew Plump almost always drove to his right. All night long we'd had Jimmy Barnes guarding him half-a-man to the right. The last thing I told Jimmy was: 'No matter what happens don't go for the fake to the left.' Well, when the clock got down to about eight seconds, Plump made a head fake left and Jimmy went for it. All of his help was on the left side and this gave Plump a chance to go right and try a shot. We had about three seconds, but in those days we weren't smart enough to take a timeout with that much time left.

"I'll tell you one thing, it wasn't anything like that movie, 'Hoosiers.' Those boys were extremely talented and deserved to win. They had the support of all but about two thousand fans and we knew we had our work cut out for us. I'll tell you another thing, if we'd won the state would've probably gone to class basketball."

McCreary tells another tale of what happened when he got home later that night. "...I'd gone home and the wife and kids had gone to bed. I was lying on the couch, drinking a coke and watching television. I wasn't paying much attention to the TV because I kept going over the game in my mind. Anyway, the movie on TV was an Italian movie and one of the actors was moving over to a desk or something. As I turned my head and began watching, the actor picked up this vase and turned it over. On the bottom of that vase were the words 'Made in Milan.' For some reason that just really set me off—I took my coke and threw it at the screen."

While McCreary and his Bearcats struggled with the pain of losing, Marvin and Milan reveled in their victory. Before they left the fieldhouse Marvin offered some consoling words to the Bearcats. Clutching the championship trophy, which was almost half his size, he told the Muncie players that he'd hated to have his boys hold the ball for so long. He then added that it was the only way they could do it. They all shook hands and then, taking the parade route around Monument Circle (backwards), Marvin and his team left for the Pennsylvania Hotel where they celebrated until early in the morning.

On Sunday the victorious Indians attended church before returning to the streets of Milan where 40,000 celebrating fans waited to greet them. The team arrived in a fleet of Cadillacs and paraded around town before ending up in the parking lot of the school where a rally was held in their honor. Bob Collins of the Indianapolis Star, the guest speaker, remembers that occasion. "Marvin told me that win or lose, they would have a rally and he asked me to say a few words. Well, figuring I'd be talking to no more than a couple hundred people, or a thousand at the most, I didn't give it too much thought—When we got down there and I saw that mob of people it dawned on me that this was quite a gathering I was about to address. I'd say it was one of the biggest thrills of my life."

After Collins spoke, Marvin took a turn at the microphone and continued in his praise for the community and the "little people" who'd helped make the team a success. Perhaps the most poignant words spoken that day came from Mary Lou, who, in one simple, sentence set the tone for the future of all involved with the Milan experience. She reminded everyone that: "It is nice to be important, but it is more important to be nice."

Monday brought the first wave of letters and telegrams congratulating Marvin and his team. Letters came from as far away as Anchorage, Alaska, as the wire services spread the news of the event to newspapers from New York to California. Most of the letters were from friends, relatives, sports personalities, and strangers. Some of these missives introduced the notion that the Indians feat had implications beyond the confines of a basketball court. A single mother from the southern part of the state wrote: "... Being a mother of four boys (the oldest just 10), I am often frightened at the thought of trying to do a good job in bringing them up to be the splendid young men I hope they will be. But my fears are soon vanished when I am so assured along the way by such fine citizens, teachers and coaches such as you. Mr. Wood, May you always be successful in building men—regardless of the score..."

Another mother wrote: "...Congratulations! Your wonderful personality is reflected in the behavior patterns of your devoted boys ... Mr. Wood you have 10 'chips-off-the-old-block' and believe me they are not splinters. You are a teacher these young chaps will never forget. Their parents must be very grateful for you."

Notre Dame's athletic director and head basketball coach, Edward "Moose" Krause wrote: "... I remember you as a player at Butler and I was very happy to see you win this great honor.. ."

Jay McCreary, coach of the vanquished Bearcats: "... Congratulations on an excellent job of coaching a most wonderful team. All of the adjectives being used cannot describe what an outstanding job you and your boys have done. We, meaning myself and the 'Bearcats' have no regrets losing to a swell bunch of 'Indians.' You won and deserved to win. True, we would have liked to get the job done, but we'll just have to work a little harder for next year. If you stay at Milan or go on to another coaching job, I personally want to wish you the best of luck and continued success. To sum it all up: It couldn't have happened to a nicer guy, and a swell bunch of kids."

Throughout the post-tournament week, letters conveying similar messages filled the town's post office. Some letters carried strange addresses such as Marvin Wood, Woodville, Indiana, or Bobby Plump, Plump, Indiana, but they all reached Milan. In addition to the letters, Western Union delivered over

200 telegrams from around the state and around the country. Never before had a basketball game at any level evoked such a passionate response from fans.

As the stream of congratulations continued, Marvin found his new celebrity status bringing him numerous requests to speak at civic events throughout the state. FOP lodges, Kiwanis groups, Lions clubs, Optimist clubs, high school assemblies, all sought to have him share his unique outlook of life. Marvin admits he expected to be asked to speak and adds that public speaking was not something that came naturally for him. "In 1953 after we'd made a trip to the final four, I had a request for me to speak at Patriot High School. I worked hard on that speech, but when it finally came time to deliver it my knees knocked and my voice quivered. I was nervous from beginning to end. In contrast, they had a group of high school students to entertain and those kids got up there and had so much fun . . . I remember coming home that night and telling Mary Lou that I would never do that again.

"The year after we won the state championship, I knew there were going to be requests for me as a speaker. I had no idea there would be so many. I made fifty-eight speeches between the end of the basketball season and the beginning of the following school year. On most occasions I brought some of the young men from the team with me. I spoke for athletic banquets, for high school booster clubs, for service clubs, and county fairs. I responded to every request and many times I did not get home until late at night."

"I generally talked about Milan and what happened to us along the tournament route," Marvin who has now become an accomplished after-dinner speaker recalls. "I'd tell folks I thought it was important to have a goal and they should be willing to work hard to attain their goals. I also explained that my faith in God played an important role in my life and in the lives of my players. Usually at least one of the boys would make a few brief comments. They all got pretty good at it."

The Spring and Summer following the winning season was a busy time for Marvin and Mary Lou. Marvin spent time with his graduating players, advising them on which of their many offers to play college ball they should accept. Bobby Plump and Ray Craft went to Butler. Gene White went to Franklin and Ronnie Truitt went to Houston to play for Guy Lewis, who'd just begun his long career there. Bob Engel, worried about his bad back and what four years of college ball might do to his physical condition, opted to forego college and begin working.

"A lot of people told me I should go to college, but my mother had done an awful lot for me and I was worried that I might further injure myself and not be able to help support her," Engel explains. "I knew that she'd worked hard and I wanted to help her as soon as I could." (Ironically, several years later Engel discovered that his back problems had come as the result of one of his legs being longer than the other—a half inch lifter in the sole of his shoe ended his back problems.)

* *

In the summer of 1954 Marvin faced yet another decision regarding his career. He had to decide whether to stay in Milan or to go to another school. "I'd given a little bit of thought about leaving Milan after the '53 season," he explains. "A small school does not make it to the Final Four often and conventional wisdom would have dictated that I leave while my 'stock was high.' Even so, I figured we'd have a pretty good year and, thinking that another good year, combined with the final four appearance in '53, would still bring me some good offers. I felt it best that I should stay with this special group of young men and see what we could do. After we won it all in '54, I just didn't see where I could take the program from there. We'd accomplished everything we could and we'd done it with a small school. With that in mind I figured it was time to look for another challenge."

"I'd always wanted to work in a larger school because, generally speaking, I'd have fewer class preparations. At Milan I taught Biology, Health, and Physical Education, which required me to prepare for three classes in addition to my coaching duties. At a larger school I'd only have to prepare for one or two classes. Larger schools also offered better salaries—But this was not a major concern of mine. In fact, Chris Volz Sr. once told me I would never leave Milan because of money. He said he'd give me a summer job that would more than compensate for any disparity in salary between Milan and a bigger school.

". . . The biggest attraction for leaving was the possibility of coaching in one of those bigger conferences—this was a challenge I looked forward to. The schools we talked to included Rushville, Anderson, Elkhart, and New Castle. We had offers from Jasper, Southport, Monticello, Valparaiso, and several colleges from Ohio and Illinois."

"Interviewing for a job after winning the state championship was quite different than it had been after losing the first game of the sectional. Elkhart, for example, was so worried about the press discovering that I was interviewing with them. They had me meet with them in a hotel in Logansport. By the time we met the rumors as to where I would be coaching next season ran rampant. I remember Elkhart's Superintendent Rice said, I hear through the grapevine that you and I are supposed to get together."

While schools wanted to keep news of their interviews with Marvin out of the papers for fear of backlash should they fail to sign him, Marvin and Mary Lou also had their reasons for keeping a low profile. "For months after that when we would be out of town someplace, we'd hear people saying under their breath 'That's Marvin Wood—isn't it?' or we'd see them pointing their finger at us in recognition. It was like having a big scarlet letter on our chests," Marvin recalls. "People who would talk to us always wanted to know if I'd be staying in Milan or where I'd be going. I'll tell you another thing—the Butler fieldhouse must seat a few thousand more people than I thought because after we won I must have met over thirty thousand people who said they were there."

The interview with Anderson provided Marvin with insight to the pressure a head basketball coach at that school could expect. "The entire school board conducted the interview," Marvin recalls. "And the superintendent would preface his remarks by saying: 'The community feels . . .' rather than 'the school board and I feel . . .' It made me uneasy hearing those words because it would be difficult to approach a coaching job under the assumption that I'd have the entire community telling me what to do. I felt uncomfortable during the interview and quickly decided Anderson, which at that time had no more talent than any of the other schools I looked at, would put me under more pressure than I would feel comfortable with."

Marvin and Mary Lou eventually decided on New Castle. "In the end I made the decision to stay in the central part of the state. Elkhart made a nice offer, but the school was much larger than any I'd ever seen and I didn't think I was quite ready to be a part of such a large school. New Castle was smaller than Elkhart, yet much bigger than Milan. They were in the North Central Conference and I looked forward to the challenge of competing in that conference. When we talked to New Castle they gave us the promise of a new facility. They'd been through a serious 'down' period, but they had an outstanding freshman team with good numbers and good size. The people were thirsty for basketball success and the situation looked promising.

"Another thing that impressed me about New Castle was the fact that they were the first ones to contact us about changing positions. They'd made their approach prior to our winning the state championship . . . The people we talked to were friendly. They were interested in what they could do for us as well as what we could do for them. The community was the same way. We received a warm reception in New Castle and Henry County."

Milan gave Marvin and Mary Lou a "going away" party as all but a few Indian fans understood that Marvin had other goals. They thanked him for his efforts and wished him success in his new position. "We'll always have a warm spot in our hearts for Milan and all of the people we came to know during our stay," says Marvin, whose face lights up whenever he talks about those magical years. "The players, my colleagues, and especially the fans, made our accomplishments all the more enjoyable."

As the waning days of the summer of '54 brought chilly nights and a hint of the coming Fall, Marvin and his family left Milan and drew to a close one of the most memorable chapters in Indiana basketball history.

8

New Castle 1954-56: In Pursuit of a Program

The position at New Castle required Marvin to do less classroom preparation, but it also presented him with a new challenge. In addition to basketball, he coached football—a difficult chore for a man who had never even been in a high school with enough resources to field a football team.

As the freshman football coach, Marvin faced a dilemma on his first day of practice. "I couldn't even tell them how to put on their equipment and I had to call in the athletic director to help us get dressed," he recalls. "I did not know much about strategy either so I watched the varsity practice to figure out what drills to have my players run. The varsity coach gave me a few plays. Things did not start well for me. On the first day of practice I had nine young men show up—one was a lineman and the other eight were backs. I'd been told that a few more would come out and that I'd probably end up with about twenty-five players. The next day a few more showed up and then the next day a few more—by the time the season was over I had fifty-two boys on the team—and I was the only coach."

The freshman Trojan football team did not win many games but, "We had a lot of fun!" Wood laughs. "I think that was one of the reasons I had so many kids coming out. They all got to play and we tried to learn a few of the basics while having a good time. I only had six plays—two or three running plays to each side and two or three passing plays to each side. Even so, I learned an awful lot about football. I learned it wasn't how big you were, or how strong you were—the most important thing was the size of the heart in the competitor. I remember one game against Anderson. They ran over our biggest kid on almost every play. This kid was about 6′3″ and he weighed over two hundred pounds, yet Anderson could run the ball right over him any time they wanted to. After a couple of quarters of this I turned to the bench and asked, 'Is there anyone here who can plug that hole?' A scrawny boy—he must have been about 5′8″ and one hundred forty pounds soaking wet—he jumped up and said, 'I can.' Well, I'd asked the question and he'd responded. I sent him in.

"I figured they'd just kill this kid, but when they ran the ball at him I heard those pads go claaack!—He stopped them dead in their tracks. I know those kids from Anderson probably went back to their huddle and told each other they were going to have to teach shorty a lesson. When they ran at him again they got the same result—claaack! This 5′8″ boy stopped them again.

That's when I decided it's not how big you are, it's how bad you want to play."

Marvin enjoyed the challenges of coaching football but quickly adds that the sport never came close to pulling him away from his first love, basketball. When he opened practices for the '54-'55 season, he discovered a lot of young men in New Castle shared his love for the game. "I think every kid who had any basketball ability at all tried out for the team," he recalls. "I had so many kids come out that I had to completely revise my practice plans." When Wood finally trimmed his roster down to the necessary number of players, he had a team with no superstars, but good size. And his players were willing to work hard. "That was something that impressed me from the start," he notes. "New Castle had good, hard-working young men. They had a strong desire to improve and be the best they could be."

Sporting a dismal 2-5 record by Christmas break, the Trojans got off to a rocky start in Marvin's first season. Things did not promise to improve soon. Over the Christmas break, New Castle would be playing in the "Big Four Holiday Tournament," which included Anderson, Kokomo, and Logansport. Anderson was ranked #3 in the state, Kokomo #4, and Logansport #9. The Trojans, with their 2-5 record, appeared to be the weakest team. But Marvin, again relishing the role of the underdog, coached his Trojans to the tournament's championship. A lot of folks from Milan were in attendance for those games and, of course, they attributed the team's success to the fact that they'd never seen Marvin lose a tournament.

"Winning that holiday tournament did wonders for our ballclub," Marvin recalls. "We turned things around from there and wound up winning the sectional."

Bob Wiles, a guard on the team, remembers positive reinforcement as the key to helping the team find confidence for that tournament and the entire season. "We'd never had a coach like Marvin. We were used to being yelled at for making mistakes, but Marvin didn't do that," Bob explains. "I remember one game in particular. We were playing Lewisville in the finals of the sectional. Late in the game I fouled one of their guys, giving him a chance to win the ballgame. Marvin called a timeout to 'ice' the shooter and when we got to the bench I half expected to catch heck for what I'd done. But all Marvin said was: 'It's ok Bob, it could have happened to anyone. I don't think he'll make them. Do you?' Seeing him so calm made me feel better and helped to make me calm too. As it turned out the kid missed both shots and I ended up getting fouled on the other end. I hit both freethrows and we won the ballgame."

Of course, Marvin was not always able to keep himself so composed, especially when one of his players would challenge his specific instructions. "The entire time I coached at Milan, I don't think I ever had a player question what I'd asked them to do. Those boys and I had an understanding that they would trust me to tell them what to do and I would trust them to do it. In my first year at New Castle I discovered that this understanding would not always exist between a coach and a team. I remember one game where we had the ball and a two-point lead with less than twenty seconds left. I called timeout and explained to our kids that we didn't want to take another shot unless it was a wide open layup. This was in the days before the intentional foul so, if we could hold the ball, we could win the game. One of the boys asked me 'You don't want us to take a shot even if its wide open?' I told him again, 'We don't want to take any shot unless it is a wide open layup.'

"Sure enough, with about four seconds left, this kid took a long hook shot from above the freethrow line—as soon as the final horn went off, I was on the floor giving that kid heck! He told me he didn't see where it would make any difference that he took a shot. I spent the weekend drawing up scenarios whereby we could have lost that game because of his ill-advised shot."

The Trojans' sectional championship capped what Marvin describes as an exceptional year. "At New Castle we were the largest school and the host for the sectional. We were expected to win. All of those little schools would get fired up to play us and it took a double overtime for us to defeat Lewisville 53-51. They had an excellent basketball team for a small school."

New Castle did not fare as well in the regional where they were clobbered by Richmond 70-57. "We played Richmond twice during the regular season, once on their floor and once on ours," Marvin recalls. "New Castle had not beaten Richmond in years, but we took it to them the first time we met. They had a coach named Art Beckner who'd coached Muncie to the state championship. After the first win he told me: 'I'll get you next time.' When we played them on their court I told our kids what he'd said and, by golly, we beat them in their gym too. After the game 'ole Art said it again 'We'll get you.' And when we played them in the regional—they got us. It was a bitter pill to swallow. They played one quarter of fantastic basketball, which was enough to get us."

1955 New Castle Varsity Basketball Team (Sectional Champs): Row 1 left to right: Charlie Thompson, Morrie Powers, Jack Razor, Kay Miller, Fred Moffitt, Herb Meredith and Jerry Walden. Row 2: Coach Wood, Don Price, Bill Richardson, Dwight Tallman, Richard Waltmire, Terry Bunner and Asst. Coach Walter O'Brien.

The Trojans ended the season at 14-11 and had made quite a bit of improvement from the time the season started. Marvin's players had learned a lot about basketball and a little bit about life. Dwight "Ike" Tallman, a senior forward, remembers what playing for Marvin meant to him. ". . . When I was a seventh grader I had a coach similar to Marvin, Von Drake. Mr. Drake got me turned on to coaching and teaching, so I was excited when I heard Marvin would be our coach . . . The mystique of Milan was a big thing to us and being able to be around the guy who'd coached that team was something special . . . But beyond that, I was taken with his smile, his enthusiasm—I don't think he ever treated anyone like a stranger. He listened to us and made us feel important. He was all of the things that made a young man want to work hard and be his best."

Tallman, who would later supplant Marvin as the youngest coach to win a state championship (1963 Muncie Central), learned a lot about the game from Marvin and was particularly impressed with Wood's philosophy on making substitutions. "Marvin worked at getting us prepared for every game—And during the game he handled himself extremely well—especially in the area of substitutions . . . He'd told us, 'Boys, when I put you in a ball game you've got two minutes to start getting the job done. I can't expect you to get in the flow within thirty to forty-five seconds. If I ever take you out without giving you those two minutes you should let me know because I will have made a mistake.' This impressed me because the players coming in need time to adjust. Few coaches seem to realize this. I'd seen coaches make substitutions and then immediately pull the kid if he made a quick mistake. Marvin's philosophy was that a player should be given an opportunity to get into the flow of the game and that substitutions are a part of the game plan. Marvin didn't simply remove a player from the game because he'd made a few mistakes—he did it because it was part of his plan to win the ball game. I agree with his philosophy and I used it with great success when I was a coach."

Walt O'Brien, Marvin's college teammate and assistant coach at New Castle, was impressed with his good friend's development from a college player to a high school coach. "We spent a lot of time discussing strategy," O'Brien recalls. "What was most impressive about him as a strategist was that he was very thorough. He had a plan and he worked it—I don't think he'd deviate a minute from that plan because he'd thought the whole thing through. He developed his program from the ground up and set it up so that the type of players he wanted would have a chance to play. He didn't leave anything to chance. What he did Monday through Thursday determined how the game was going to turn out on Friday."

As Marvin's abilities to work with his students became known to the community, the praise from parents soon followed. Marvin is especially proud of the thanks he received from Mabel Mukes whose son, Victor, played for Marvin during his second season at New Castle. "Victor was a talented basketball player," Marvin recalls. "He was about six foot tall, and he could jump up and grab the rim with both hands. Victor had been in trouble with the law. He'd spent some time in reform school—and he was black.

"In many communities there'd be a ruckus over giving such a young man a spot on the high school basketball team, but

Victor earned his spot. As long as he stayed out of trouble I was glad to have him play for me...He stayed out of trouble and became a valuable member of our team. When it came time for me to leave New Castle, his mother made a special effort to get in touch with me. She thanked me for giving her son an opportunity to earn back his position in the community by being a member of the basketball team---It was thanks such as Mabel's that helped me to realize my efforts with the boys had effects far beyond the basketball court."

Aside from his players and friends from the coaching ranks, Marvin began to develop friends in the community too. The teachers at New Castle were friendly and outgoing and once they'd gotten over the fact that Marvin was a bit of a celebrity, they began to invite him and Mary Lou to social activities before or after ball games.

"When we first moved in people had expectations of one kind or another—especially since we'd won that state championship the year before," Mary Lou recalls. "I remember one lady had a son who was out for the basketball team and she came by one day and said, 'We would like to be friends with you and Marvin, but we feel that you'll have to make the first move because if we make the first move people will say we're just trying to keep our son on the team.' This was new to me because most of our social activities had been more or less tied to basketball games and beyond that we did not do much except with our families and friends from Butler."

Marvin and Mary Lou enjoyed New Castle, but as the school board began to "drag its feet" regarding plans to build a new gymnasium Marvin began to question the community's commitment to developing its basketball program. In addition to what he perceived as a flagging enthusiasm for a basketball program, his next season's basketball team was decimated by unfortunate incidents—all of which led him to begin looking for another position.

"Between the end of the basketball season and the end of the school year, we lost three of our most promising sophomores," he recalls. "One of them got kicked out of school for smoking in the school cafeteria; another was in a group of young men who got caught breaking into a service station; and another got a girl pregnant and had to get married. This was going to make my second year a major rebuilding year. With no movement on the new facility thoughts came to mind that maybe I'd better start looking around..."

When Wood read of a coaching vacancy at Peru he figured he ought to give them a call to see what they might have to offer. "Marvin had told me he was thinking about trying to find a new position and when the job at Peru opened up he asked me what I might think about living there," Mary Lou recalls. "I remember the night he sat down to call them. Just before he picked up the phone he received a call from J. Everett Light, who was Superintendent at Rushville. Mr. Light had been hired as the new superintendent at North Central in Indianapolis which had yet to open. He told Marvin that North Central would not open for another year and asked him if he would be interested in the head basketball coaching position when the school opened."

Wood accepted the position at North Central. "I'd come to New Castle under the pretense that a new basketball facility would be built, but it seemed to me the plans regarding that facility were pretty much at a standstill. It also occurred to me that if I had plans to leave, it'd better be pretty quick before the Milan magic was forgotten," explains Marvin who, in the meantime, faced a difficult final season as head coach of the Trojans. "Having lost three of my most promising players, I knew we were in for a long year. We had a terrible season (6-14). Even so, the young men on that team were a great group of competitors and I could tell they would improve in the coming years." When Wood left New Castle at the end of the '55-'56 season he left behind a maturing, talented ball club and a "feeder system" which would provide a parade of talented basketball players for years to come. Walter O'Brien, who stayed at New Castle as an assistant coach for several years after Marvin left, feels Marvin laid the groundwork which has helped the basketball program become the powerhouse it is today. "... When Marvin came to New Castle the basketball program was in bad shape," relates O'Brien." They had no feeder system except for the one junior high school team and no continuity between the high school coach and the junior high. Therefore, one of the first things Marvin had to do was to build a feeder system.

"He worked with the school board, the principals and the superintendent to develop what he called a 'double team' schedule. This involved splitting the talent at the junior high and freshman levels into two teams at each level. This permitted an opportunity for twice as many kids to play. Two seventh, eighth, and freshman teams, provided twice as many kids for the reserve and varsity teams at the high school level.

"Marvin left without ever coaching the kids who came out of this program, but the guy who came after him, Randy Lawson, had plenty of talent to chose from. In fact, when I left New Castle (two years after Marvin left) I got a call the next season from Randy and he wanted to know how to 'cut' talented kids from the team."

Ironically, New Castle started construction on the new facility during the year after Marvin left. The basketball program eventually developed into one of the better programs in the state. "If I would have stayed at New Castle for one more season," Marvin grins and shrugs his shoulders, "I'd probably still be there."

If Marvin could have known the difficulties he would soon encounter at North Central, he might not have left.

9

North Central 1956-65: Frustration at Work— Happiness at Home

Family portrait 1961.

The move to Indianapolis and North Central brought Marvin the most difficult seasons in his career—but it also provided some of the most rewarding years of his life. Fortunately, this change in coaching positions came at a time just before young Douglas started kindergarten. Both Doug and Deidre started their school years in the North Central area where the Woods built their first home and settled in for a long stay.

"We were impressed with the teachers and schools of Washington Township," Mary Lou recalls. "When Doug started school he had just nineteen kids in his class and the teacher was assisted by a mother/helper every day. During his first year at St. Luke's Douglas did quite well on his aptitude tests. In fact, he scored so much higher than his classmates his teacher thought there must have been some mistake. So she kept him after school and tested him again with much the same results.

"Later, when enrolled at John Strange elementary, Doug did just as well and again, we believe his teachers had a lot to do with his success... With Dee it was a little different—she didn't get the specialized attention Doug got in kindergarten. Her class had more students and no mother/helper. Even so, she was a bright girl and a hard worker. We were very pleased with her academic progress."

When Doug became old enough to be involved in sports, Marvin, like most fathers with active sons, found himself coaching a range of different teams. In addition to basketball at North Central, he coached Little League baseball, YMCA basketball and football and several church teams on which Douglas played. By the time Doug was in junior high school it became apparent he would not follow in his father's footsteps as a quick little basketball player. Perhaps one of the only similarities between the Doug and his father was that Douglas also broke his collarbone while playing on the seventh grade team (Marvin accomplished this feat as a junior in high school.).

"Douglas saw the game well and he was coachable," Marvin recalls. "But he wasn't quick, nor was he as tall as the other boys. I thought he had more ability to play football than basketball. His approach to sports was different from mine. In the beginning I think he enjoyed playing because of the friends that he made more than he enjoyed the competition. I think that changed when he had a little success—especially in football and wrestling. After that I think he really began to enjoy the competition."

Marvin and Mary Lou enjoyed raising their children. Despite the demands of his coaching career, Marvin was able to find time to spend with Doug and Dee. "I sometimes wish that I'd taken them fishing more or something like that," Marvin confesses. "In retrospect it seems that a lot of the time I spent with them was as a coach or observer."

Finding a balance between work and family is a problem all working parents must confront, but the dilemma is doubly difficult for a coach and educator because his or her job requires doing many things that parents do—namely paying attention to young people. Marvin found a balance between home and work, but also gives his and Mary Lou's parents a great deal of credit for helping raise Dee and Doug. "Doug was the apple of grandpa Henley's eyes," Marvin recalls. "When Doug was young his grandfather, who worked as a general contractor, would pack Doug a lunch bucket and take him along to work. They were great buddies." Dee and Doug also had fun at the Wood's farm in Fountaintown where they learned about farming and farm animals.

Deidre remembers a wealth of pleasant childhood memories. "Despite the fact my father was gone a lot, I'm one of those lucky people who was raised in a stable household. If I remember correctly, dad was still working on his master's degree during those early years at North Central so there were times when dad was not around until late in the evenings. I remember mom saving dinner until eight or eight-thirty on some of those nights because she thought it was important for the family to eat meals together.

"There was a time in my life when I resented the fact that dad spent so much time away, but in retrospect I think he did a good job of paying attention to us. We had other benefits too. For example, we went to basketball games with mom for as long as I can remember and I was always pleased to be able to sit in the first row next to the cheerleaders. On those occasions I don't think any girl in the gym felt as lucky or more special than I did . . . Occasionally dad took us to practice with him too and even though he didn't pay a lot of attention to us while practice was in session, I think we felt kinda special just by being there.

". . . We went to church on Sundays which was always a day to spend with family. About twice a month we'd go to our grandparents after church for lunch and that was always fun because they lived on a farm where there were lots of things to do. Holidays were another important time for us. This might seem strange, but I enjoyed Memorial Day more than I did Christmas. Memorial Day was special because we'd get up early and go to my grandparents where grandpa, dad, and his brothers would take us kids fishing. We'd fish for hours. I don't remember catching many fish, but it was fun to listen to dad and my uncles talk about all the things they'd done around that fishing hole when they were young. Afterwards we'd have fried chicken and strawberry shortcake and play in the yard while the adults listened to the Indy 500 on the radio. We did that every year.

"Church played an important role in our family too. Through our lessons there and the example set by my parents I learned to treat others as I would like to be treated. At Christmas time, for example, mom and dad taught us to be thankful for what we had and to help others. One year this notion was brought home to us in a real sense. Through our church mom and dad got the name of a young girl from the inner city who needed clothing. Before Christmas we went downtown to take this girl to dinner and to do some Christmas shopping. She was my age and I remember Doug and I were so surprised to find that she'd never been to a restaurant. Mom and dad did things like that to teach us about the world around us.

"Another of my favorite memories involves my father and ballroom dance lessons Doug and I took. At the end of the year our instructor held a party where the girls' fathers would dance with them and the boys' mothers would dance with them. Dad was always comfortable on a basketball court or speaking in front of a group of people, but he was completely out of sorts when it came to dancing. He was nervous as we sat there watching Doug and mom—put him at a sporting event and he's just fine, but if you dress him up, shine his shoes and tell him that he's going to dance, well, that was really putting the pressure on. While we were waiting our turn a little girl whose father had not come came up to dad and asked him if he'd dance with her. He tried graciously to get out of it, but, being the good sport that he is, he relented and did the best he could—and, as always, he did it with a smile . . . I wish I could be more like him."

* *

During his nine years at North Central Marvin renewed many

old acquaintances from his playing days at Butler. Bill Shepherd, Jim Rosenstihl, Charlie Maas, and Jimmy Doyle all coached schools in the area so Marvin and Mary Lou spent plenty of time with them and their families. Yet, while friends and family helped make Marvin's years at North Central pleasant ones, his tenure there as basketball coach was difficult. In the school's first season they lost eighteen games, including a fifteen-game losing streak. Marvin's inexperienced team, which had no seniors and only two juniors, captured a small measure of satisfaction by knocking off their first two sectional opponents before falling to eventual champ, Thorntown, by a basket.

"I'd taken the job at North Central because I relished the challenge of being able to build a program from the ground up. The area around the school was growing and the community looked like a utopia," Marvin recalls. "They had high hopes for athletic success and the many hoops on the garages throughout the area gave me the impression there would certainly be some promising athletes coming into my program. Even so, our first year was tough. With no seniors, few juniors and a major league schedule I hoped for the best and prepared for the worst—and let me tell you, it got pretty bad. We ended the season at 3-18.

"I remember at one point we were 1-15 and one of my players, Dan Kelly, came up to me and said, Coach, I don't know if it's worth it. We spend a lot of time and a lot of energy during the week, yet every weekend we end up losing.' I told him if he felt he was wasting his time it would probably best if he turned in his uniform and found something else to enjoy. He assured me he wasn't ready to quit and figured we had another win somewhere but he was beginning to wonder where.

"We did not win another scheduled game and entered the sectional tournament at 1-17. Playing at the Zionsville sectional, we drew a team with a 12-8 record for our first game and we beat that team by ten points. The next night we played Lebanon, who was favored to win the tournament, and we beat them too. After that game I was walking down the hallway and Dan Kelly came up to me all sweaty. He picked me up and threw me in the air exclaiming: Coach! coach! Its all worth it!"

The Panthers, posting a remarkable turnaround, went 13-8 in their second season. Even so, Marvin could see trouble down the road. Wood thought it essential to have a feeder system similar to the one he'd developed at New Castle, but J. Everett

Light, the superintendent of schools, would not permit him to develop one.

"Talent was never going to be a problem at North Central," Marvin explains. "We always had good talent, but chemistry was often a problem because our kids were simply not as prepared as those from the schools we played . . . I wanted a developmental system, but when I went to Mr. Light and asked him if I could have one he said no. He felt the community wanted to stress academics. He said they wanted a good athletic program but they would not let 'the tail wag the dog.'

"I had a great relationship with Mr. Light, but on this issue I did not agree with him. I didn't disagree with putting academics first, but we had our English department and our math department coordinated between the elementary and middle school and the middle school and the high school. We had continuity between those programs. All I wanted was the same thing in my basketball program. I asked him if such an approach was good for academics why would it not be good for athletics? He remained firm on this issue stating that we were not going to do it as long as he was in charge.

"Our excellent talent allowed us to catch up with the other schools with developmental programs, but it was like fighting with one arm tied behind your back. Most of the schools we played had feeder programs and their kids were coming in way ahead of ours at the tenth grade. By the time ours caught up we would lose them to graduation. If we'd been even at the tenth grade level we could have made even more progress."

Wood adds that he had opportunities to hold clinics with his lower-level coaches, but he could not insist that they do the same things he was doing with the varsity and junior varsity teams. "I could ask them to do what we were doing, but in coaching you generally do what you know best and a lot of these guys had been high school coaches and had their own way of doing things. Afterall, why should they spend the time to learn something new? They weren't making big money and they already had something they figured would work."

Despite the limitations placed on his program, Marvin's teams were competitive. In his nine years at North Central he had several good teams and four winning seasons. After having so much success with Milan he'd hoped the larger schools would offer him more opportunities to win the big tournament. Unfortunately, this was not the case. It was during this time that

Marvin began to appreciate his '54 team even more. "They had talent and chemistry—especially chemistry," Wood explains. "As the years passed and my teams simply could not make it 'over the hump,' this concept of chemistry seemed to be the problem. How the players got along with each other or how well they listened to my instructions and got along with me— those things had more to do with success or failure than talent."

In addition to what Wood describes as chemistry, the level of competition in the North Central Conference, in Marion County and in Indianapolis was much higher than it had been anywhere else. "I love good competition," Wood confesses. "And we had good competition almost every night out. Even the small schools were tough."

By the time the late 50's and early 60's rolled around, many of Marvin's innovations such as the "cat and mouse" and the "zone trap" were now part and parcel of every coach's arsenal. On many occasions Marvin watched his teams get beat with the types of defenses or offenses he'd earlier helped to bring into the game. Yet, he did not grow discouraged. He simply continued to work with the tools that had brought him success, making adjustments when needed, encouraging his players to perform to the best of their abilities.

Though he did not win so much as a sectional at North Central, he did win respect and admiration. The parents of one player once told the newspapers: ". . . I don't care if we never win so many games. So long as we have a coach who teaches and treats the boys like Marvin Wood does." The down side of the Milan experience was that Marvin was unable to get his teams to play at such a lofty level, but on the up side he did much to prepare the young men on his teams for their lives after basketball. Remembering what Mary Lou had said on the occasion of the '54 championship, "Its nice to be important, but its more important to be nice," Marvin lived up to that motto through the good times and bad.

Mike Chapman, who played for Marvin at North Central, admired Marvin for his consistency in handling each of his players, no matter what their level of talent. "He taught us to have goals," Mike recalls. "He treated us all the same. No player was any more important than the others. Once our best scorer was goofing off before practice, taking shots from fullcourt or something and Marvin walked into the gym and caught him. 'Son,' he said, 'if you haven't got any more respect for a basketball than that, then I think you should leave.' This guy looked at Marvin and walked off. Our star player walked right out of the gym and Marvin started practice as though nothing had happened. That was the way he was. No player was more important than the team."

Chapman, who later went on to play for Tony Hinkle at Butler, relates another story from his college days. "Hinkle used to tell us, 'Guys, in the game of basketball there are two kinds of players—dribblers and bouncers. I'm going to tell you the name of the best dribbler I've coached and the best bouncer I've coached and as soon as you hear their names you'll know the difference between a dribbler and a bouncer—Buckshot O'Brien was the bouncer and Marvin Wood was the dribbler.' He'd go on to explain that O'Brien, who was one of the schools all-time leading scorers, would bounce the ball around trying to create an open shot while Marvin would dribble around trying to find the open man. If what he said is true, Marvin coached a lot like he played."

Marvin had two successive years at North Central which he describes as his worst and best. "The 1960 season was probably the most disappointing season of my coaching career," he relates. "I thought we had enough talent that year to win the state. We had quickness, size and depth. I had twelve basketball players and all were capable of playing on the starting five.

"Before Christmas we were in the top twenty in the state and we'd lost only one game—that loss was against #1 ranked Kokomo. They beat us with a last-second shot. Over Christmas break, however, something happened to our team. I have no idea what it was, but when those young men came back from Christmas they were a different basketball team. The chemistry changed and things turned completely around. Some of our problems may have been related to injuries to two of our best players. One of our starting forwards hurt his right shoulder and was out for a couple of weeks. When he came back he was not the same. We also lost our center who hurt his back. The loss of those two players should not have hurt as as much as it did.

"Some attitudes seemed to change and I don't know what caused that to happen. After Christmas break my players became more concerned about 'self' rather than the team. Our shooting went sour. The choices we made on the floor were not sharp. We didn't play as well defensively. Try as I might I could not shake that team out of the doldrums. We had a terrible second-half of the year and lost early in the sectionals. After an 8-1 start we ended the season with a 14-10 record. It was probably the most disappointing season of my career.

"The next season we lost all but three players from the previous year. Mike Chapman, Dick Best, and John Kelly, had very little varsity experience, but they were good young men with a lot of heart. It looked as though it was going to be one of those long rebuilding years. But, while the talent was not nearly as good as the 1960 team, the attitudes were great and the chemistry was excellent. Those kids worked hard to overcome their weaknesses and they were a group of what I called 'over-achievers.'

"In 1961 we won the Marion County tournament. I don't think anyone thought we'd even win our first game. We were not supposed to be the upper echelon of the County that year but we finished the season at 16-6. That team, too, was a mystery. They just fit together and got the job done."

By the end of Wood's seventh season at North Central he began to get restless. Superintendent Light showed no signs of changing his mind about the developmental program Marvin wanted and, in fact, had suggested Marvin ought to begin to think about moving out of coaching and into administration. ". . . He'd made the suggestion [about becoming an administrator], but I wanted to make that move when I was ready. I didn't feel as though I was ready to get out of coaching just yet," says Wood who did interview for a job in New Albany at the end of his eighth season. After visiting the school, which is located in the southern end of the state, Wood decided he didn't want the job. "They would not give me more than a one-year contract," Wood recalls. ". . . And I really didn't want to move my family that far south."

He stayed at North Central for another year then decided to leave for a head coaching position at Mishawaka High School in the north central part of the state. "George Oberle, our head baseball coach at North Central, knew I was not happy about not being able to get the developmental system the way I wanted it," Marvin explains. "I thought with a developmental program we could be a state power every year. I was frustrated. George knew Dick Brainerd in Mishawaka. They were frustrated, too, because they were having trouble finding a coach who would set up a developmental system. George got the two of us together . . . They wanted to build a program and paid their coach better than North Central—aside from that, the Mishawaka school system was in a program emphasizing the development of educational ideas. The school system was among the best in the state. They had a lot of things that I wanted so I decided to make the move."

Wood made his first visit to Mishawaka the day after the horrible tornadoes of Palm Sunday 1965. "Seeing that destruction was a humbling experience," he recalls. "It amazed me to see mature trees pulled right out of the ground, roots and all." Little did he know that in the coming years, just as nature's winds had tried the foundations of those trees, the winds of fate would twist and try the foundations of his faith.

10

1965-1969: Mishawaka-Shelbyville and a Change in Careers

Family portrait 1965.

Moving from their home in Indianapolis was difficult for the Wood family. The nine year stay in Indianapolis represented the longest time they'd spent in a community and the years there had been productive. Dee and Doug received their elementary education in Indianapolis and the Wood family had become an active part of the community.

During Marvin's tenure at North Central, his reputation as a teacher and motivator of young men and women brought him respect and admiration—just as his coaching innovations had done during his earlier years. He was disappointed that his teams had not done better, but felt no pressure from the community and was content with the work he'd done in his nine seasons. ". . . I can't say I felt pressure from the community about the success of my basketball program. I could understand if people were not happy with the way things were going, but in so far as pressure—I guess I'd have to say the most pressure I felt was that which I placed on myself . . . You ask yourself: 'Why am I not getting the job done on the level I'd liked to.' But I've always been able to tell if my teams were improving, if they were playing up to their capabilities. I felt if the kids were playing their best and the team performed up to its potential, then I was getting the job done.

"Besides I had a pretty good idea as to what I thought was holding us back at North Central. I thought a developmental program would give us a chance to be a state power every year. I looked forward to having the opportunity to build such a program at Mishawaka."

Mary Lou also looked forward to the opportunities made available to Marvin in Mishawaka, and looked back in appreciation of the years they'd spent in Indy. "Indianapolis had been a good place to live and, while we'd moved a lot during Marvin's career, I was grateful we had not moved while the kids were going through elementary school. It was as good a time as any to make a move because Doug would be starting high school, which meant a change in schools anyway. Dee would be in eighth grade. She was outgoing and I didn't think she'd have any problem making the adjustment.

"Mishawaka is a smaller community so I thought we'd feel right at home there . . . Anyway, when Marvin and I were married we both understood we'd be moving from time to time. We agreed where ever we lived we would make it our home and we would like it."

"We tried to look ahead instead of behind," adds Marvin. "Once a decision is made second guessing is nothing more than an exercise in futility."

Douglas and Deidre were split in their opinions about leaving Indianapolis. "I think Doug appreciated the education he was getting in Indianapolis," Mary Lou recalls. "He was a little apprehensive about moving."

Dee, on the other hand, welcomed the change. "I was really excited," she recalls. "We'd lived in the same house for eight years and I was ready for a change. In Indianapolis we lived in one of the nicest parts of town and most of my classmates came from affluent families. I wasn't insecure about my dad's work or anything, but a lot of times my classmates made a big "to do" about their parent's financial success as doctors and lawyers and I just got tired of it.

"Moving to Mishawaka was neat because they made a big deal about getting dad to coach there. They ran his picture in the paper and said things about Milan. Going in, I felt we were wanted there."

"The adjustment was easy for me. I made more friends during my eighth grade year at Beiger than I'd made in the nine years we lived in Indianapolis."

Marvin, with the blessings of the school administration and the help of high school principal, Walter Thurston, began immediately to work on a developmental program, starting in the elementary schools and coordinated through the high school program. "We split the freshmen into two teams and ran coaching clinics for the middle and elementary coaches," Marvin explains. "This required quite a commitment from the administration because they had to add several coaching positions which was going to cost some money. It also required sacrifices from the coaches in the lower grades. They had to learn the Hinkle system then teach it to the kids. We held clinics for them to teach the drills and so forth—this meant that they had to commit quite a bit of time to learning and then teaching this system..."

Ralph Causey, an elementary school coach during Wood's seasons at Mishawaka, described the developmental program this way: "I think a lot of us had mixed emotions about the program. We understood the concept of trying to achieve continuity from the elementary schools on through to the high school, but many of us were concerned about the amount of time it would take to teach the Hinkle system to younger kids. We weren't being paid much to coach and before Marvin came most of us would simply find a few plays and we'd tried to make basketball fun for the kids. Using the fundamental drills and teaching the Hinkle pattern demanded a lot more preparation and patience.

". . . I still use the Hinkle pattern and I think it's a good system. But when I look back at my years at Mishawaka, I must admit that it was frustrating to see talented kids who I'd spent hours teaching get cut from the high school team. Sometimes I wondered if the developmental system was really worth the time and effort. Ultimately, I suppose it was, but it also was a source of frustration for many of us who worked it from the ground up."

While Wood was pleased with the beginnings of his developmental system, he struggled with a varsity team that had little talent and a tough schedule. "We had little talent that first year," Wood recalls. ". . . Not much height, and little quickness—but those kids were willing to run the soles off their shoes to get the job done. They were coachable and did everything I told them. But those things could only carry us so far. Without talent we simply were not going to win many ball games."

The Cavemen won their first two ball games and then fell apart. ". . . We used a full court press in our first game and we won going away. We won our second game doing the same thing. After that the wins were few and far between. In fact, we closed out the season by losing our last twelve games in a row. In those twelve contests we played eight teams that were ranked in the top twenty. I remember one game against 8th-ranked LaPorte we scored nine more field goals than them, but still lost—We just weren't very lucky either."

The 5-16 finish was one of the worst years Wood had as a coach. As he looked ahead to his second season he couldn't see things getting that much better. "That first season was tough—and I couldn't see much talent coming along for the next few years. This had me concerned because I was already beginning to feel a little bit of pressure.

"After the first year Mr. Thurston, the principal, came around and asked me what he could do to help us speed things up. I told him there were some things you just couldn't hurry and we had a lot of talent coming up in the lower grades. He stood there for a moment then asked: 'Are you telling me to get the hell out of here and mind my own business?' His question surprised me. Mr. Thurston had a gruff way of doing things so I thought long and hard before I answered. I told him that was not what I meant and that I was glad he was concerned about the program and wanted to help. After hearing this he said: 'Yea, well I can take hint!' then he turned and walked out, slamming the door behind him. Nothing more was said but I began to wonder what might happen if we had a couple more bad seasons. I knew that the during the next years we were not going to have the talent we needed to compete against the competition in our conference. I worried I might suffer through a few tough years and then get the rug yanked out from under me as the kids in the developmental program reached high school."

Shortly after the confrontation with Mr. Thurston, Mary Lou received a call from her sister, Rita, who told her that their mother had suffered a heart attack. "Yes, that was quite a shock," Mary Lou recalls. "Mother was fortunate not to die. We were concerned because she didn't seem to be able to recover. She was in the hospital for a long time. She had pneumonia and the doctors weren't encouraged that she would get better. I'd been making trips to see her whenever I could and, fortunately, an opportunity arose where we could move to Shelbyville allowing us to be close to her."

Mary Lou needed to be close to her mother and Marvin had second thoughts about the security of his future in Mishawaka. At the same time, Shelbyville, a community not more than twenty miles from Mary Lou's parents, had an opening at their high school for both a basketball coach and an athletic director. All of which made Marvin decide to leave Mishawaka for Shelbyville—he'd also decided to take the athletic director's job rather than the coaching position.

Wood's decision to change careers did not come as a result of doubts about his abilities as a coach. He made the change out of concern for his future. "I've always maintained that a good coach will know how well his teams can play. If my teams had consistently failed to play at the level I thought they were capable then I would have had to change some things or perhaps consider the possibility of getting out of coaching. All along I felt I'd done my best as a coach and the inability of my teams to go further in the tournament had no bearing on my decision to become an athletic director. I made the career change because I'd recently turned forty and wondered how long a guy ought to coach before he tries his hand at something else. I'd continued my education at Ball State to get a Administrator's Certificate and I figured if ever there was a time to take advantage of that additional education, this was it."

"Dutch" Thurston and the administration at Mishawaka lobbied hard to get Marvin to stay. This impressed Marvin because he'd thought they'd been disappointed with his work. Even so, Mary Lou's desire to be with her mother and the opportunity available at Shelbyville made it impossible for Marvin to stay. So, after one dismal season at Mishawaka, Marvin and his family headed back to central Indiana.

This abrupt change in address was easily accommodated by Doug. Dee, however, had enjoyed her year so much she was reluctant to move again. "I wasn't interested in moving again," she confesses. "I got angry about it and promised myself I would make mom and dad as miserable as I could for awhile..."

This move came at what was proving to be a difficult time for Marvin and Mary Lou. "We talked it over with the kids and they didn't seem to mind that we were going to make another move," Mary Lou recalls. "It was funny because when Marvin told Mr. Thurston we were moving, Dutch said, 'Well, we don't mind losing you, but we sure as hell hate to lose that kid [Doug]. Its not often we get kids as good as that.'

"The move to Shelbyville was not nearly as hard on the kids as it was on us. My mother was still ill, but she was beginning to show signs of getting better. Then, not long after we moved, Marvin's mother died suddenly which really hit us hard. She was a special person in our lives and we'd looked forward to having her around to see the kids involved in their activities."

Marvin, who gives his mother credit for helping him become the person he is today, was deeply affected by her death. "My mother was an important influence in my life and in the lives of my brothers. After she died our families didn't get together as much, and that sense of family has not been as strong."

**

Despite Dee's earlier misgivings about the move, she and Doug fit right in at Shelbyville high school, quickly distinguishing themselves as excellent young musicians. "Shelbyville high school had a performing arts program called 'show group' and both Dee and Doug became a part of that group," Mary Lou recalls.

"The kids were talented musicians," adds Marvin. "They must have gotten that from their mother because I'm not much when it comes to performing. Dee was the only freshman girl selected to perform in that group and Douglas became such a good singer that he and three other classmates formed a group called 'The Gateway Four,' which eventually did some concerts with the once-popular Kingston Trio."

In addition to their musical talents, Dee and Doug found fun and success during their high school days in Shelbyville. "During the first months I was dedicated to making dad's life miserable," Dee recalls. "But after I got over the fact that we were now living in Shelbyville, I got along pretty well. I got teased a lot by people who'd known dad and his brothers when they'd played ball for Morristown. I guess they must have given Shelbyville fits, but I didn't know what they were talking about.

While Marvin enjoyed having the opportunity to be at the same school as his children, Dee and Doug sometimes found the arrangement somewhat awkward. "Fortunately, I never had him as a teacher," Dee recalls. "Having him around was not so bad until I started dating. I don't think it would have been so bad if he'd just been a teacher—but he was the athletic director and a lot of the guys I dated participated in athletics. So, if we stayed out late or anything I think they were more afraid my dad might find out than I was.

"We understood we weren't going to be able to cut up a lot with him around. I remember a 'Sady Hawkins' dance where mom and dad were chaperones. They got all dressed up—it was a little embarrassing."

While Doug and Dee made a successful transition into Shelbyville high school, Marvin found the duties of his new career to be as challenging as those he'd found in coaching. "Being an athletic director was really a challenge," he recalls. "When we came to Shelbyville I walked into a situation where a couple of positive things greeted a newcomer. We had competitive schedules and loyal fans. Shelbyville was strong in basketball, football, and wrestling."

"One of the things I noticed right away was that our football team was one of the best equipped in the state. Every player had a new uniform and new equipment. This got me to thinking that things were really good here Shelbyville and they probably had a lot of money for athletics. Of course, later I discovered that the new equipment had been ordered just before I arrived. I had to do some juggling here and there when the bills came in after the football season was over. It was one of many learning experiences for a new A.D."

Wood was impressed with the professionalism and dedication of the various coaches on his staff and with the enthusiasm the community displayed towards the school's athletic program. He enjoyed most every aspect of his job—except for one, his duties as ticket manager. From the horror stories shared with him by Cale Hudson at Milan, Wood was somewhat familiar with the trials and tribulations endured by the person in charge of distributing tickets. Even so, he was not at all prepared for the maelstrom created by jilted fans.

"I discovered we had fifty four doctors receiving passes to our athletic events, most of whom performed no service whatsoever for the school," he recalls. "I reduced that number down to just the people who were providing services for the school. While such a move made sense to me it was not an easy thing to do— being the ticket manager was a pain in the fanny. I probably had more criticism and threats of my handling of tickets over the three years that I was there, than I had in forty years of coaching. I learned a lot by being a ticket manager. I learned that you can't win and you can't trust anybody. People will try to take advantage of you in any way they can.

"I had people threaten to blow the front porch off my home. I had people threaten to whip me—and I knocked myself trying to make everyone happy. One time we were scheduled to play Columbus at their place. They normally sent us two hundred and fifty tickets to sell. I knew we could sell two or three times that number so I called Bill Stearman, the A.D. at Columbus, and told him if they had more tickets to sell to send them to me so our people wouldn't have to drive down and take the chance of making the trip without getting a ticket. He sent me seven hundred fifty more tickets. I had one thousand tickets for our people and I thought I was doing something good. On the day those tickets went on sale we had people lining up at two in the afternoon to buy them. By the time the ticket office opened at 3:30, the line ran all the way around the building—At about four o'clock this big guy came walking in and when he saw the line he came by the office and said: 'If I don't get a ticket, I know somebody who's going to get whipped!' He was looking right at me when he said it.

"We had excellent teams and a big demand for tickets and it seemed to me that I was always in trouble over tickets. This did not sit well with me at all because I've always been the type of person who tries hard to please people, but when it came to tickets, there was just no way of doing it."

Wood worked three years as an athletic director before deciding to return to his first love—basketball. "Being an athletic director was a fun challenge," says Marvin. "I was busy all of the time. I met many nice people. Working with the kids was fun, but sometimes dealing with adults got to be a problem. . . That's really the biggest reason I decided to get back into coaching—I enjoyed working with young people."

Another factor which contributed to Wood's decision was what he saw as a growing inequality in the compensation for athletic directors compared to that of coaches. "In the late sixties and early seventies many new sports were added to high school programs," Marvin explains. "Girl's athletics were beginning to play a larger role and some of the minor sports were becoming more important. All of this meant an increase in work for athletic directors, but it was becoming increasingly clear that there'd be little increase in pay. In the meantime, coaches—especially those involved with high-profile sports such as basketball and football—were making more money. I interpreted this to mean that school corporations thought less of A.D.s than they did their coaches, so I figured it might be time to get back into coaching."

In a twist of irony Wood ended up back in Mishawaka. "A good friend, Dick Powell, told me that the coaching position was open up there," Marvin recalls. "I applied for the second time, but after leaving three years ago I did not think they'd want me back. However, they did call me for an interview and I thought the interview went very well. Walter "Dutch" Thurston who by then was the assistant superintendent of instruction, conducted the interview and I thought he asked great questions. He and Max Eby, who replaced me as coach, had done a great job in keeping the feeder system intact and I could tell Mr. Thurston was concerned about the school's basketball program and wanted to get the right man to make it successful.

"Unfortunately, I did not get the job. They selected someone else. Then, in the middle of August right before school started, I got another call from Dick Powell. He told me the guy they'd hired had backed out and he asked me if I was still interested. I told him I was interested in Mishawaka, but I didn't think Mishawaka was interested in me. Dick assured me they were. He said Mr. Firmani, the high school principal, would make the decision. I called Frank Firmani who asked me if I wanted the job. I accepted."

The timing of the Mishawaka offer and Wood's acceptance coming so close to the beginning of the school year posed several dilemmas for the Wood household. They did not have their home in Shelbyville up for sale, nor had they any idea where they would be living in Mishawaka. In addition to this, Dee had another year of high school to complete and the dilemma arose as to whether she should finish it at Shelbyville or Mishawaka. "... We finally made the decision to let Dee stay in Shelbyville and graduate," Marvin recalls. "We did this primarily because she had many good friends and was involved in a number of activities which probably would not be available to her at Mishawaka."

"It was a difficult decision, but I wanted to stay." says Dee "In retrospect, however, I was lonely that year and, while I think my dad was trying to let me do what I wanted, this was one of those cases when it probably would have been better for me to go with my parents."

Mary Lou wanted Dee to make the move to Mishawaka. She felt Dee was outgoing enough to make new friends and find other activities for her senior year. As was often the case, however, she trusted Marvin to make the final decision. Perhaps the most important factor in Marvin's decision was the fact that they did not know where they'd be living in Mishawaka.

"Given the circumstances we faced and the concern about being separated for the better part of that first year, I think the move to Mishawaka in 1969 was probably the most difficult we'd made," recalls Marvin. "We'd always been a close family and now for the first time we were going to have to spend time away from one another. I don't think that sat well with any of us."

11

Mishawaka 1969-80:
Years of Triumph,
Years of Tragedy

Photo Courtesy South bend Tribune

The return to Mishawaka started in turmoil. While Marvin spent the first six weeks of the school year living with friends, Mary Lou and Dee stayed in Shelbyville until their house sold. When it did Mary Lou moved in with her mother while Dee stayed at the home of Virginia Goodley Jones, a friend of the family in Shelbyville. "It was a difficult time for all of us," Mary Lou recalls. "I was obligated to work at Chrysler until December and when we finally found a home in Mishawaka basketball season was about to begin. Our jobs and moving our belongings from one place to another left us with little time for anything other than travelling between Shelbyville and Mishawaka. We weren't able to enjoy Dee's senior year and did not get to visit Douglas at DePauw as often as we wanted."

By Christmas, Marvin and Mary Lou were back together in a beautiful two-story home which overlooks the St. Joseph river. Dee was doing fine in Shelbyville and had decided she to pursue a education degree at Ball State. Douglas had made the Dean's List in his first semester at DePauw and his letters home were full of love and concern for his family.

Mary Lou's move to Mishawaka found her without children for the first time since her husband's first season in French Lick. "As I look back I realize that I was pretty depressed with the kids gone," she recalls. "We'd moved in and after everything was cleaned and in place, there really wasn't much to do. And, while I hate to admit it, I did spend quite a bit of time on the sofa just staring at the walls. I think one of the things that helped me break out of it was our choice of a home. Whenever I'd get to missing people I'd sit at the table and write letters. From where I sat I could see the river and the snow covered trees hanging out over it. The view was simply gorgeous. That old river has been a comfort on many occasions."

Marvin's first season back as a basketball coach found him reaping the benefits of Mishawaka's feeder system which in his absence had been nurtured by Mr. Thurston and Max Eby. "Max did a lot of positive things with the group of young men I inherited during my first year back," Marvin recalls. "He and Mr. Thurston had worked hard with the coaches from the elementary and junior high schools. Their work was beginning to show in the type of kids we were getting into the program.

"My first year back I had the Gautier twins; Gary and Gray, and Dan Fowler, a solid center. We had a 14-10 season but probably would have done even better if not for the fact that

Dan tore up his knee playing touch football prior to the basketball season. The injury required surgery so he didn't play for about half the year. In his first game back we played Elkhart. They were ranked #2 in the state—and we whipped them."

While Marvin gives his predecessor, Max Eby, and the developmental system much of the credit for the improvement in Mishawaka's basketball program, Eby, who'd coached the team during Marv's three years at Shelbyville, sees things differently. "In order to see what Marvin did for Mishawaka's basketball program, I think you have to look at both the history of basketball at Mishawaka high school and the basketball programs in and around the area," Eby explains. "... To make a long story short, Mishawaka had little in the way of a basketball background. They'd last won a sectional in 1955 and had but one conference championship in the last twenty years. I believe Marvin changed all of that during his first season... The developmental system was part of what he did, but he also brought enthusiasm and a never say die' mentality that stuck with the program even after he left.

"Mishawaka had a difficult schedule. South Bend always had a couple of highly rated teams; Elkhart and Michigan City still had but one high school and many of the schools just south of Mishawaka such as Plymouth and Logansport had well-established feeder systems. To be honest, I was surprised Marvin's first team was even able to win five games. But beyond that he sold those kids on basketball. Even after they had a horrible year and knew that Marvin would be leaving, those kids worked hard all Summer to become better basketball players. In just that one year here, Marvin convinced a lot of people that Mishawaka basketball could be competitive.

"Unfortunately, towards the end of my three seasons I found expectations to be much greater than the talent here would allow. For example: We had people who felt our program could win a state championship in the next several years—Never mind that we were in a tough conference and played in a sectional that generally featured at least two of the top ten teams in the state—we had people who expected this program to win a state championship. Well, that was just a little too much pressure for me. I love a challenge as much as the next guy, but I was looking at a sectional or a regional as a place to start—not the state championship. As a result of these expectations I decided to get out of coaching."

Eby further explains that the reason Marvin was contacted so late about coming back to Mishawaka was because the coach they'd picked over Marvin had believed what he'd heard about the expectations for the program, but when he came around to see the kids playing in the summer he decided that he no longer wanted the job.

When Marvin came back he brought with him the "Hinkle system" and combined it with a fastbreak which utilized the sidelines instead of the middle of the court. "We needed a fastbreak to beat the bigger teams who'd simply park their big guys under the basket and deny us the lane," says Wood. He gives Don Cromer, one of his assistant coaches, credit for developing a fastbreak with the outlet pass to the sidelines.

"It occurred to me that most of the traffic after a missed shot usually came towards the center of the court," Cromer explains. "So, I figured if we asked our back men to release to the side, then the outlet pass would go away from the traffic and give us an open passing lane to the other end." Cromer is quick to add that if it were not for Marvin's willingness to listen to his assistants such innovative thinking would not have become a part of their program. ". . . That's one of the great things about Marvin," says Cromer, an assistant to Wood for over twenty years. "He's always listened and that helps to make me want to do the best job I can. I won't say he's taken me up on all of my suggestions over the years, but he has made me feel like I'm an important part of the team."

Understanding a medium-sized school system such as Mishawaka's would probably never have as much talent as the larger schools in the area, Wood directed the attention of his program towards developing intelligent, team-oriented players. Such an approach was not always appreciated by the "downtown" coaches who often saw what they considered to be talented ball players cut from Marv's teams. "I probably did make a few mistakes along the way," Marvin admits. "But I knew what kind of players I wanted on my teams and I was generally quite pleased with the ones I kept.

"I was fortunate to get back into that program when I did," he adds. "I'd seen some talent in the middle grades when I left and those boys were now making major contributions to the program."

Marvin uses Lou Mihailovich to illustrate the type of player he wanted in his program and what a developmental program can do for a marginal player. "Lou was not more than an average player when I first saw him as a freshman in high school," Marvin explains. "In fact, he didn't even make the freshman team. But we had a second freshman team we called the 'yanigans' and Lou wanted to be a basketball player so he played on that team. By having an opportunity to have someone work with him, and by working hard, Lou became an excellent team player. What he lacked in natural ability he made up for in smarts and heart. Lou started for us during the 73-74 season—a season during which we went 20-3 and ended the year ranked #4 in the state."

In 1973-74, after many years of frustration, Wood finally found himself coaching a talented basketball team that generally played the way he wanted them to play. The '73-'74 squad featured some of the best players to ever play basketball for Mishawaka High School. The team was anchored by Mike Needham, who at 6'8", was the tallest player Marvin ever coached. In addition to Needham, the Caveman's frontline included Tim Kizer, a 6'5" all-conference forward, and Marc Gautier, whose twin brothers played for Marvin in earlier years. The starting five also included Lou Mihailovich and Scot Shaw, two star athletes who were also members of the Caveman's highly-rated football team.

This talented squad had a decent, but not so spectacular first half of the season. They lost an early game to cross-County rival Penn and came away with several close victories which could have easily gone the other way. Over the Christmas break, however, they distinguished themselves as one of the best basketball teams in the state. Playing in a holiday tournament at Carmel, the Cavemen upset #6 ranked Franklin, which had gone to the state finals in the previous season and featured Don and Jon McGlocklin. After spotting the Grizzly Cubs a 20-10 lead, the Caveman came back to win 66-56. They did it on the strength of their defense which held Franklin to just seven out of twenty-five field goal attempts in the second half. The victory gave Wood's charges a tremendous amount of confidence as they lost only one other game—an overtime defeat against South Bend Adams. Unfortunately, that loss cost them the Northern Indiana Conference title.

Sporting an 18-2 record and ranked #4 in the state, the Cavemen entered the sectional at South Bend as the co-favorite with South Bend Adams. Twenty years had passed since Wood's famous Milan team of 1954 and the sportswriters could not resist making comparisons between that championship team and the Mishawaka ballclub which was enjoying the school's most successful season. Wood, too, saw similarities. "We had a great bunch of kids at Milan—good students, good Christian young men and they worked well together. We lost two regular season games that year, one in overtime and another by a wide margin—all of those things were true of that Mishawaka team too."

However, unlike the Milan team of '54, the Cavemen were unable to advance out of the sectional. #7 ranked Adams beat them for the second time in as many meetings. The Eagles got out to a twenty-point lead early in the game and, try as they might, the Cavemen were unable to catch them. "That was a very difficult loss for me to swallow," Wood confesses. "I made a mistake in not having our boys use a full court press earlier in the game. We didn't go to the press until we were way behind, but while we were using it we were getting back into the ballgame. I didn't think we could stop their quickness, but we could. It was one of those situations where I underestimated the ability of our kids which made losing just that much tougher."

Tim Kizer, one of two seniors to graduate from that team and an all-conference forward, remembers that loss and the long bus ride back to Mishawaka. "... The loss against Adams was really tough. We'd been down so far and had fought back so hard, but in the end we just didn't quite have enough ... During the bus ride home I thought a lot about how that game would be my last in a Mishawaka uniform. I thought about Coach Wood and what a wonderful inspiration he'd been to me over the past years. As we were getting closer to the high school the bus was quiet, but we had this thing—we called it the 'tarzan tradition' which we did on the way back from all of our away games. As we got close to the high school, all of us guys would start chanting 'tarzan, tarzan, tarzan ... ' until Coach Wood would lean out from his seat in the front of the bus and give out this 'tarzan yell.' Granted, it was a somewhat silly tradition, but it was just one of those inside things for the team and all. Anyway, as we got close to the high school a couple of guys started chanting 'tarzan' and pretty soon we all joined in. Coach Wood didn't do anything for a long time and then, just as we drove up to the high school, with tears in his eyes and in a strained voice—for one last time he gave us that tarzan yell. I guess that's a silly thing to remember, but it left an impression on me."

Despite the sectional defeat, Mishawaka had its most successful season since 1955. The team's 20-3 record was the best in the school's history and the fine season earned Marvin the District 1 Coach of the Year award. Beyond the '73-'74 season the future bode well for the Cavemen. Marvin lost only Lou Mihailovich and Tim Kizer to graduation and had several good players to replace them.

Mishawaka's 1974-75 campaign would prove to be the third-best of Marvin's career career. The two starting spots vacated by Mihailovich and Kizer were filled by Chuck Alexander, who'd been a standout on the football team and Audie Freeman. The development of Freeman was a pleasant surprise because he was neither exceptionally quick nor tall—". . . but, boy oh boy, could he shoot that ball!" Marvin recalls. "That young man made himself into a great shooter. He could shoot from fifteen to eighteen feet like it was a layup. On our fastbreak we could run him to the corner because he could hit from there just as easy as he could under the basket—and teams wouldn't cover him out there. He made a major contribution that year."

Ironically, Mishawaka had its best year in football in 1974, too. The football team's success caused problems at the beginning of the basketball season. "Back then the IHSAA had a rule that anyone who was going to play had to be involved in at least five practices," recalls Mike Needham. "The football season ended just a couple of days before our first game and Coach Wood had us practicing twice a day so Scot Shaw and Chuck Alexander could get in their five practices. I remember them soaking their blistered feet after practice and it took them at least a couple of games [to get in synch] with the rest of us."

Mishawaka won its first two games that year before being hammered by Penn 68-50 at Mishawaka. The Cavemen recovered from that loss and went on to post their second consecutive twenty-win season. Along the way they lost only two more regular season games; one to arch-nemesis South Bend Adams 75-74 and another to Michigan City Elston 78-76. The Adams game gave the Cavemen a great deal of confidence despite the loss. "Even though we lost that game, I think we came away feeling as though we could beat them," recalls Audie

Freeman. "They had 7'2" Glen Sudhop, 6'7" Val Martin, 6'8" Mark Riesinger, and 6'7" Darryl Ashby. They were a lot taller than us. We played that game at Adams in an uncomfortably warm gym and they needed a bucket right at the end to beat us. We figured if we could get them on a neutral court we might be able to beat them."

Freeman adds that the Cavemen were able to have success against taller and more talented opponents because of the various offensive and defensive strategies Marvin had taught them. "You had to be smart to play for Marvin," says Freeman, who was the Cavemen's leading scorer in 1975. "We used five or six different defenses and on offense we could either run the fastbreak or setup in the Hinkle and patiently look for the right shot."

"Yes," agrees Mike Needham, "you could not be physically or mentally lazy if you planned on playing for Marvin. He got the absolute maximum out of each of us. I think he had every one of us playing as close to our potential as possible."

By the end of the season the Cavemen earned a #9 ranking, but inevitably would have to face #2 South Bend John Adams in the sectional. "We'd been ranked #4 during the previous season and Adams had been ranked #7," Marvin recalls. "We'd lost in '74 and we were looking for revenge in '75.

"I thought I'd made a mistake in '74 by not using our full court press so in '75 we started the game with a press and it was successful. We ran the fastbreak to avoid letting them get their big men underneath the basket. We executed well both offensively and defensively. We shot well. We passed well—and we led them from start to finish. In fact, during the last half of the game we shot mostly layups. They had big Sudhop and our center, Mike Needham was a little quicker up and down the court. We devised a little setup off the freethrow line so that when they were shooting freethrows one of our guys would 'pick' Suds while Needham took off running to our end. I think Mike got at least a half-dozen easy layups off of that little adjustment. We'd done our homework on them and in the end it paid off."

The sectional title was Mishawaka's first since 1955 and suddenly this football community was excited about its basketball team. "I'd say they were the best team I'd ever seen at Mishawaka," recalls Dave "Daisy" Klein, one of the basketball program's most ardent supporters over the years. He describes the 1974-75 team as one of the most entertaining squads he's seen. "Marvin had this reputation as someone who'd stall and run what might be considered a slow, boring offense—but that was never really the case. They ran the fastbreak better than any team I've ever watched. More often than not they'd get a rebound and bang! The ball would be at the other end of the court with the same guy who'd gotten the rebound shooting a layup—and many times they'd do it without taking a single dribble.

"Prior to Marvin coming to Mishawaka this was pretty much a football town," Klein adds. "We had basketball fans, but I don't think anyone thought we'd be in a position to win a sectional or anything. But by the time Marvin came back the second time folks started to believe that we could win in basketball too . . . 1973-76 were great years for Mishawaka high school basketball fans."

1974-75 South Bend Sectional Champions: Front row left to right: Tom Gosztola, Randy Schlundt, Mike Needham, Scot Shaw, Chuck Alexander and Jeff Done. Second row: Randy Powell, Brian Eberhardt, Steve Kobold, Coach Wood and Team Physician Dr. Paul Macri. Third row: Asst. Coach Don Cromer, Freshman Coach John Taylor, Steve Schlundt, Audie Freeman, Jon Thuerbach, Marc Gautier, Jim Plonski, Junior Varsity Coach Jerry Shaw, Bob De Vreese and Trainer Herschell Bryant.

The 1975 South Bend regional featured several of the state's best big men. In addition to the Cavemen's 6'8" Mike Needham, North Judson had 6'9" Fred Eckert, Valparaiso's center, Don Rose came in at 7'2" and Michigan City Elston had 6'7" Albert Johnson, who could "jump right out of the gym." The Cavemen drew North Judson in the afternoon contest and the two teams put on a great display of patient, error-free basketball.

Mishawaka got behind right away and could draw no closer than four points by halftime. In the second half, however, they improved their marksmanship (they shot 51% for the game) and moved ahead 44-40 in the third quarter. In the fourth quarter Mishawaka out-scored Judson 20-12 to ice away a 64-52 victory. "We did not get off to a good start against North Judson," Marvin recalls. "But we did manage to stay close and I thought we were playing well. When we caught them in the third quarter, I felt we were getting stronger and stronger . . . Fortunately, we were able to put them away in the fourth."

Unfortunately, the victory did not come without a cost. During the last three minutes of the North Judson game, Mike Needham hyper-extended his knee. His status for the evening's contest was questionable.

In the afternoon's second contest Michigan City Elston got out to a big lead against Valporaiso and then had to hang on down the stretch to win 66-55. Thus, the regional final would pit Mishawaka against Michigan City. "With a healthy Mike Needham we had an excellent chance of winning," recalls Marvin. "With Mike in there we were able to completely dominate the game. Unfortunately, he was limping around on his bad leg and we didn't know how long he'd be able to play. We asked him several times if he needed to come out—but he didn't want to because he was afraid that if he let his knee get cold it would stiffen and he would not be able to play. We left him in the game, but City got wise and started running plays right at him—Mike fouled out early in the third quarter and then we were in trouble.

"We took a timeout after his fifth foul and I remember telling our boys that Michigan City thought they had this game won. I told them it was up to us to prove them wrong."

Despite the physical and psychological loss of their tallest player, the Cavemen continued to battle. They ran the fastbreak when it was available and patiently worked their offense when it was not. Behind an excellent twelve-point effort from

Needham's replacement, Steve Kobold, the Maroonclads led 67-63 with 1:40 left in the game. On the verge of winning the school's first regional in four decades, the Cavemen, who had only committed seven turnovers in the afternoon contest, committed two quick turnovers which the Red Devils turned into baskets—sending the game into overtime.

Neither team could score in the first overtime. But during the second overtime another Cavemen turnover gave Michigan City a two point advantage. The Red Devils continued to shutout Mishawaka and came away with a thrilling 71-67 double overtime victory.

Despite the loss Marvin and his team received praise for the way they handled themselves. ". . . It was largely through the sensational efforts of Steve Kobold and the other starters who gave a little bit extra that we were able to get that game into overtime," Marvin recalls. "When it looked like things were really dark those kids played with their hearts on their sleeves. I received many compliments about the way our kids played and behaved during the tournament and, despite the fact that we lost a game we probably could have won, I was proud of those young men."

Despite the regional loss, the '74-'75 season will always be special to Marvin. It was during that year that the then forty-eight-year-old coach was elected to the ndiana Basketball Hall of Fame. "I cannot find the words to describe the way I felt about being given such an honor. I suppose one of the things that made it even more special was the fact that I received word of my induction from a good friend and college teammate, Charlie Maas—and another good friend, Bill Shepherd was inducted that same year.

"I've always thought that just being able to play and coach was reward enough," says Wood. "As a young man growing up on a farm in central Indiana I dreamed of having the opportunity to play and coach. For the last forty years I've been living that dream.

"In the back of my mind I figured I might have a chance to make it into the Hall of Fame, but I figured that might come years down the road—I was surprised it happened in my first year of eligibility. It's a great honor to be a member of such a distinguished group."

1975 was also the year Dee got married. "1975 was indeed an eventful year," Mary Lou recalls. "Marvin was having two of his best seasons since we'd left Milan. He was named Coach of the Year in '74 then was elected to the Indiana Basketball Hall of Fame in '75. Later that year Dee married Craig Juday in a lovely ceremony. She looked so pretty and he so handsome— Marvin and I were both pleased and proud."

While 1975 brought the Woods a great deal of joy it also brought them a great deal of sorrow. As they enjoyed Marvin's success and the new horizons brought on by Dee's marriage, they struggled with Douglas, who'd slipped out of step with the rest of the family. At the time Marvin was enjoying renewed success in his career he and Mary Lou were placed in a private hell by their only son whose life was being destroyed by drugs and hopelessness. "Yes," Mary Lou recalls, "we sure needed some 'ups' to take care of the downs."

Marvin and Mary Lou had first become aware of a change in Doug during the summer between his freshman and sophomore years of college. "As we look back now, it's easier to see where the changes came and where we might have been a little more attentive," explains Mary Lou. "Between Doug's freshman and sophomore years he'd been having some emotional difficulty because he and his high school sweetheart were no longer dating. We were living in Mishawaka and he took a job down in Shelbyville and lived with my mother. Apparently, he'd started hanging around with some guys who had the reputation of being drug-users. My mother said something about it, but we didn't give it much thought because Doug seemed to be doing well. His grades were good and he'd always been good about not getting involved with things which might hurt him.

"Later that summer we went down to see his group perform with the Kingston Trio. We both felt something was wrong with him on that occasion. He seemed a little distant and anti-social. We talked about it a little bit and figured it might have something to do with his breaking up with his girl friend. But when he came home for Thanksgiving that year he was not the same Doug we'd seen go off to college."

"We thought he was maturing," Marvin interjects. "We thought he might be trying to develop his own values and that maybe he was testing some of the things we'd tried to teach him. Our parents did not interfere too much after we left their home and I think we tried to treat Doug the same way. We figured he was on his own and we didn't want to make his visits unpleasant with a lot of questions about the way he dressed and how he wore his hair and his attitudes and so forth."

The Woods later discovered that the change in Doug's behavior and dress was partly due to the fact that he'd been using drugs. They believe he turned to narcotics to help improve his performance as a racing bicyclist. "Doug worked at his bicycling and he'd often mentioned that one of the people he trained with had said that certain narcotics would improve his performance," says Mary Lou. "We don't know if he started using drugs because of this or not . . . We'd also had several arguments about the legalization of marijuana but there was a lot of talk like that going around in the early seventies and we just didn't give it too much thought.

"We became even more concerned during his senior year of college because during the Fall semester he called home and said that he was having trouble with school because he couldn't remember things. He wanted to quit and come home. We agreed that he would check to see if his scholarship would still be good if he quit. He checked it out and told us that if he quit before the first of November he would not lose his scholarship. We told him to make the decision and he never mentioned it again.

"His grades were not off that much at the end of the semester, but when he came home for Christmas things were not good at all. He couldn't even get himself organized enough to do his shopping. He'd go and look, but he wouldn't buy anything. We knew something was terribly wrong, but we didn't say anything."

"It never even entered our minds that it might be due to drugs," adds Marvin. "We figured we'd brought him up right and just could not believe he'd be messing around with anything so dangerous."

Marvin and Mary Lou admit they continued to deny that Doug might be using drugs right on up to the time Doug admitted to it. And they still find it hard to believe his involvement was as extensive as it apparently was. "Yes," Mary Lou admits, "we were a classic example of parents who simply refused to believe their child would be involved in such a thing. We didn't know much at all about drugs or about the way people behaved when they were using them."

At the end of Doug's senior year, Marvin, Mary Lou, and several members of the family went down to Doug's graduation. They found him in ill-spirits. In addition to his moodiness and disregard for his personal appearance, Doug's last semester grades were the worst he'd received in his fours years. Even so, his GPA was well above 3.5 and he quickly found employment at Miles Laboratories in Elkhart. Living with his parents, he seemed to adjust well to his new-found employment. But then, after about eighteen months he began to have trouble at work. He was often late or did not show up at all. On other occasions he got into arguments with his supervisors or other people in authority.

It was during this period that Marvin and Mary Lou began to suspect Doug might be using drugs. "We'd asked him once and he said no,'" recalls Marvin. "But then Mary Lou found some marijuana in his closet and Dee told us about some things she'd heard. In the meantime Doug continued to insist that his problems were not related to drugs, but wanted to see a doctor because he was having problems. He started seeing one of the best psychiatrists in the area, but then he refused to work with him. It was at this time we began to believe that his change in appearance, attitude, dress, and social values was due to something other than psychological problems."

Shortly after Doug's visits to the doctor a close friend of his from college committed suicide. In subsequent discussions about the reasons for this young man's death, Marvin and Mary Lou learned that Doug had taken the hallucinogen, LSD. Then, once while Mary Lou was doing the wash, she found syringes in Doug's pocket. This evidence convinced Marvin and Mary Lou that drugs were indeed a problem in Doug's life. "Finally, we talked to some mental health authorities who'd counseled Doug," Marvin recalls. "They confirmed he was using drugs and that this was a problem Doug would have to deal with himself."

Meanwhile Doug's problems at work got him transfered, then dismissed. "He blamed things on the people over him," says Mary Lou, "but in the end he simply was not showing up for work or when he did show up he wasn't doing what they wanted him to do." She adds that they did not always react well to the problems Doug began to pose.

"We didn't want to accept what was happening. We tried to deny that drugs were the root of the problem. We wanted him but I can't say that we really knew how to help. We knew he'd used drugs, but we didn't believe he'd developed a habit. Our refusal to believe this let the problem get way out of hand."

As they watched their son slowly slip into hopelessness the

Woods were now desperately concerned and tried to get Doug into counseling. "It hurt us to see someone who'd been on the top of the ladder going down, down, down," says Marvin. "Our natural response was to help, but when Doug started to become more and more violent—we began to wonder if he was even going to be able to stay in our home."

Doug's violent confrontations with his parents eventually led them to force him out of their home. "On one occasion I was reading the paper and Doug came right through the paper and at me," recalls Marvin. "It's a good thing I was still fairly athletic because he might have strangled me to death that night. I was able to get my legs under him and grab a handful of his hair. We had several knock-down drag-outs like that."

Doug had become a shell of the son Marvin and Mary Lou had raised. They did not know how to help him and lived in increasing fear of his violent outbursts. Then one night while Marvin was speaking to the local booster club Doug came home and did something that would lead the Woods to have him committed to a mental hospital. "He came by that night and I could tell that he was really depressed," recalls Mary Lou. "He went into the kitchen to get something to eat and I offered to fix him something. We went back and forth for a while and he was on this kick about how selfish everybody was and how nobody wanted to give anything to anyone else and so on. This was partly because he didn't have any money and he knew I wasn't going to give him any.

"Anyway, he was gripping about this and that and somehow ended up with a butcher knife in his hand. He stood across from me in the family room with his foot propped up on the chair and he stared at me. I don't recall what he said next, but I do recall that I was not frightened. 'Douglas,' I asked, 'what are you planning to do with that knife?'

"'I don't know yet,' he answered. And then I said, 'You're my son Doug I love you and I'm not afraid of you. I'm not afraid.' He waved the knife and said: 'I ought to just let you have this!" I told him he could go ahead and do that because I knew I was right with God and if he should take my life he would pay and pay and pay. He stood there for about ten minutes and then moved into the other room where he turned and threw the knife at me. It missed me, broke a lamp, and hit the wall.

"Then I was scared. I was scared because I didn't know if I could get out the front door before he caught me—but when I went for the front door he didn't chase me." Mary Lou fled to the neighbors where she telephoned the police.

Knowing that their only son was a threat to their lives left Marvin and Mary Lou shattered and frightened. They knew they had to do something drastic, but still wanted to help Doug as much as they could. After much deliberation and discussions with Doug's doctors and counselor they decided to have him committed to a mental hospital (Drug treatment centers were not yet available). They believed by doing so they would isolate Doug from them and give him an opportunity to sort things out in a controlled environment. The process of getting him admitted was hampered by red tape and Doug was not cooperative, but eventually was admitted.

His stay at LaRue Carter helped Doug get his life straightened out—but only temporarily. He was soon back to the drugs and alcohol which, in turn, made him irrational and prone to violence. Doug's susceptibility to the effects of drugs and alcohol may have been worsened by hypoglycemia. Hypoglycemia is a condition causing too much sugar in the blood stream and can easily be controlled with a proper diet. In fact, when Doug watched his diet and stayed away from alcohol he always seemed to get better. Even so, he simply could not make himself stay away from the drugs and alcohol.

"When Doug was not on one of his binges he and I had some great heart-to-heart conversations," Marvin recalls. "He'd tell me it was as though Mary Lou and I were separated from him by a fence. He knew he wanted to get over that fence, but somehow he just couldn't quite make it. He told me he'd started in with the drugs because he thought it was a game he could control. He would then admit the game had gotten out of control and now it was controlling him.

"But even after those heart-to-hearts he would inevitably end up going out with the wrong people and then he'd drink or use drugs and the cycle would start again. I don't suppose we'll ever know exactly why he kept going around in that vicious cycle, but I often suspect when he was away from the drugs and his mind cleared up a bit he thought about how he'd damaged his mind and would never be able to be the bright young man he once had been. I think just knowing this depressed him and he didn't want to think about it so he'd go back to the chemicals to erase the memory of how things once were.

"Despite all he'd said and done, we hurt to see him

floundering as he did. And we tried everything—spent a small fortune on counselors and doctors and sat through hours of counseling. We tried diets and prescription drugs, just about anything then available. Yet, he seemed to fight us every step of the way. Doug had gotten involved in a situation that was far too big for him to handle and he was reluctant to let anyone help him."

Finally, after years of struggling with his problems, after countless tears and numerous nights of anguish and frustration, Douglas Wood died in a motorcycle accident. "They called us from the hospital at three o'clock in the morning," recalls Marvin as he fights back the tears that come so easily when he remembers those difficult days with his son. "They told us our son had been in a bad accident. As we got ready to go I told Mary Lou that they had not told me he was going to be ok—all they'd said was it had been a bad accident. When we got to the hospital they told us his motorcycle had struck a truck then got caught on its back end. The motorcycle caught fire and Doug had been burned to death. They would not let us see him."

Doug's untimely death brought mixed emotions to Marvin and Mary Lou. They were devastated by the loss, yet found a sense of relief. "Yes," whispers Mary Lou, "because of all we'd gone through—it was a relief. We finally knew for certain that this terrible part of our life was over."

"It was a relief in two ways," adds Marvin. "It was a relief for him—he'd been through a hell worse than the one we'd been through. I can remember on more than one occasion where he'd prayed to God to take his life if he could not go back to being the way he'd been before.

"For Mary Lou and me it meant an end to the sleepless nights, an end to the fear in which we'd lived for far too long... I don't know, maybe this is a cruel way to look at it, but I felt that maybe his death was an answer to his prayers."

"We'd pray that we did not know how much longer we could handle the situation," adds Mary Lou. "Maybe Doug's death was God's way of saying That's enough.'

The ordeal with Doug has made the Wood more sympathetic to people facing similar situations. "Before all of this happened I don't think we realized that bad things can happen to good people," says Marvin. "Now we realize you can do your best to be good parents, you can try to correct your mistakes and show a child all of the love you have—and still sometimes things will go wrong."

The Woods add that while they were aware of the dangers of drugs, they never imagined it would affect their lives. "We denied it for a long time," admits Mary Lou. "Even now, I find it difficult to believe such a thing could happen to my child. And yet it did—but I don't think its anything to be ashamed of . . . I think the biggest mistake we made was not seeking help sooner."

Marvin and Mary Lou believe their faith in God and their love for each other helped them through the crisis. "Our faith grew in leaps and bounds," admits Mary Lou. "If not for the fellowship of Christian friends and the knowledge that a greater power was watching over us, I don't know how we would have handled things."

As a result of their experience the Woods have been more than willing to work with people suffering from similar circumstances. "I figured we could respond to the tragedy in one of two ways," says Marvin. "We could become bitter and complain about this terrible injustice we'd suffered, or we could go out and share our experience with other people to try and help them avoid some of the pain we've lived through—And let me tell you—everytime we get an opportunity to help someone it makes us feel as though maybe all of our suffering had a purpose."

* *

In the years following Doug's death, Marvin gave a great deal of thought to changing directions in his career. He thought he might like to be come a counselor. While the experience with Doug played a role in his thinking, the decline in talent in Mishawaka's basketball program, combined with pressure from school board members, also helped him to come to the conclusion that it was time to either change schools or change careers.

"Talent was extremely thin for a few years and I could not see more coming up," explains Marvin. "We were short and slow and I knew we were in for a string of long seasons. In my next-to-last year we had a 2-19 record and in the two games we won we beat the only teams on the schedule that had talent equal to ours. Things did get better during the next year. We were 12-10, but I couldn't see much light at the end of the tunnel."

"After that 2-19 season we began to hear some comments," adds Mary Lou. "People suggested that maybe Marvin was getting too old or maybe he'd lost his touch. And, as is often the case throughout the state, members of the school board started getting involved. And when those board members start giving advice on how to run the team, or who to keep, well, you know its time to start looking around. Its amazing, Marvin had been in coaching for over thirty years and yet some of these board members would act like it was they who'd had all the coaching experience. When that started happening and we saw little talent coming up Marvin thought he'd like to try being a counselor—so he made the change."

"Yes," agrees Marvin, "I suppose you could say confidence was waning and the high school was going to have an opening for a counselor in the next year, so I talked it over with a couple of people in the administration and they were encouraging. They told me if I wanted to retire from coaching they would help in any way they could to get me prepared for the counseling position."

Marvin decided to make a change. His preparation for the transition included four college courses related to counseling. He admits that going back to school at age fifty-two was difficult.

"I had not been in the classroom as a student for over twenty years . . . I was older than most of my fellow students. I think the closest person to me in age was about thirty-two. When it came to opinions mine were often quite different from those of my classmates. As time went on, however, either I changed or they changed because towards the end of the semester we were agreeing with each other more often. I think I learned from those young people and I think they learned some things from me."

After completing his course work Marvin retired from coaching and embarked upon a new career in counseling. He had mixed emotions about leaving the coaching profession. "I think it was a smart move," he offers. "But there were times when I'd be walking by the gymnasium and hear those balls bouncing—it doesn't take much to bring memories back when you've coached as long as I had."

While Marvin contemplated the challenges of a new career and relished the memories of his days as a coach, Argos, a tiny school of 271 students, snuck through the state tournament and made it to the final four. The year, ironically, was 1979—exactly twenty-five years after the Milan Miracle of '54. Inevitably,

Marvin was asked if an Argos state championship would diminish some of the "Milan Mystique."

"We've had it for twenty-five years and its been twenty-five beautiful years," said Wood in an interview with Steve Warden of the Fort Wayne News-Sentinel. "I think its time for somebody else to have the spotlight . . . We've been in the news nearly every year since it happened and I can think of no better team to replace us than this 28-0 Argos ballclub."

Unfortunately, Argos did not win the state championship in 1979, but the "Milan Mystique" would continue to be an inspiration for all those small schools to continue to try.

12

New Challenges

07 October 1990 - Marvin meets with President George Bush and Vice President Dan Quayle.

Plunging into his new duties with the same enthusiasm he'd formerly devoted to his basketball teams, Marvin made a successful transition from coaching to counseling. "I wanted to learn as much about the school's programs as I could," recalls Marvin. "So, I spent time in every classroom; made a visit to every club; watched practices in all of the various sports; and reviewed all of the resources the school had to offer. This information was quite valuable because prior to becoming a counselor I had no idea as to the scope of a high school curriculum."

"Marv was the best counselor I've ever worked with," comments Robert Smith, principal at Mishawaka throughout Marvin's years both as a basketball coach and counselor. "He was so good that it became a problem for us because everybody wanted Marv for a counselor. As a counselor he was a consummate professional—just as he was when he coached. He had a way with kids and he could handle parents well too."

"He was especially good with kids who needed a friend to talk to," adds Jeanette Davis, who assisted Marvin with his on-the-job training. "Students were often hesitant to share their problems with some of the rest of us counselors—we had the tendency to be a little less patient—Marvin, on the other hand, was extremely patient and seemed to able to win the confidence of young people. He gave a lot of his time. In fact, after he got to feeling a little more comfortable with the job, he developed 'group sessions' which he held after school. He didn't feel constrained by time. If somebody needed more time he gave it, and yet he could tell if he was being taken advantage of too."

Marvin gives Jeanette much of the credit for helping him make the successful transition. "She was like a mother to me," says Wood. "I must have asked her a hundred questions a day for several weeks and she was patient in answering every one of them."

While Marvin enjoyed his work, he was surprised and somewhat dismayed to discover the wide range of problems teenagers must face. ". . . I had students tell me about parents who were drug pushers or sexual abusers. I had kids tell me about being threatened by their mother's boyfriends. Others, through peer pressure that sometimes bordered on being down right vicious, were being tempted by drugs and alcohol. There were things we could do to help remove the threat or to help them resist temptations, but it was difficult to help them with the emotional scars.

"Young men and women who have been abused and are afraid often suffer from low self-esteem. As a counselor and maybe one of the few adults in their life with whom they could discuss their problems, I felt I should try to give them as much attention as I could—but with so many kids needing so much attention, it was impossible to do the job as well as I would have liked to do it."

Aside from dealing with the various personal problems encountered by students, Marvin's duties also required him to help students make decisions on what they should do after high school. "That wasn't always easy," he recalls. "Parents often had unrealistic expectations for their children. It was sometimes difficult to reconcile those expectations with the child's progress in school. So much emphasis is placed on going to college, but some young men and women can do just as well by not going to college. For example, I was impressed with the opportunities being offered by the armed services. They offered expensive and extensive training that could help young people become contributing members of our society. My main theme was to encourage young people to stay in school and do all they could to prepare themselves for life after high school."

In 1982 Marvin, who'd come to terms with his life without basketball, was asked to take over the girl's program at Mishawaka. "John Taylor, a close friend, fellow coach and an important part of my basketball programs, had been coaching girls basketball. In the Fall of 1982 he suffered a massive heart attack," recalls Marvin. "Fortunately, he lived, but it would be months before he'd be well enough to come back and coach—so Bob Smith and Max Eby asked me if I would be interested in taking over. I told them that the girl's game was something new to me and I didn't know many of the girls on the team. I took the job because I love a challenge and wanted to see if I could get the best effort out of those young ladies.

"During our first practice I talked to the girls and told them this would be a new experience for both of us and we'd have to do our best to make it work. Fortunately, it worked out beautifully. I didn't know much about our girls so I started out by running a fullcourt press and substituting four or five girls every five minutes or so. I thought I'd do this for two or three games until I could decide who were the top six or seven girls. But the original plan worked so well I decided to use it for the entire season. We ended the year at 22-2."

Marvin saw differences between the boy's and girl's game and immediately set about trying to take advantage of them. "I noticed the girls were poor passers and weak perimeter shooters. We worked on those things to get better and we tried to exploit them as weaknesses in our opponents. On offense we ran a basic set called the 'shuffle' which emphasizes short passes and interior shots. Nonetheless, I had my girls work on both passing and perimeter shooting every day in practice. On defense we pressured our opponents all over the floor."

Wood coached Mishawaka to the NIC championship, and to sectional and regional titles. He had a chance to win a state title in both girl's and boy's basketball. A tough team from Heritage, however, ended that hope and closed Marvin's career as a high school girl's coach with a semi-state defeat. "I had a lot of fun that year," he recalls. "It had not been that long since we'd been hearing those comments about how the old man had lost his touch. But we didn't hear much of that kind of talk during that '82-'83 season . . . I found out that the young ladies are just as competitive as the boys, only they listened a little better. They wanted their day in the spotlight and they were willing to work hard to get there. I never heard any of those girls say 'I can't,' I heard a lot of them say 'I'll try.'"

Wood's success led Sharon Versyp, Mishawaka's all-state guard, and Karen Phelps (Digger's daughter) to ask him to help with their AAU team, which they hoped would be able to compete in the Junior Olympics, held that Summer at Notre Dame. In order to get to the Olympics the young women would first have to make it through a state tournament. With Marvin as coach they won the state tournament and placed eighth in the Junior Olympics.

"AAU tournaments are usually double elimination," explains Marvin. "We were competing with thirty other teams and had to face the team that won it in our first game. We lost and had to fight our way back through the losers bracket. The young ladies worked hard and we ended up in eighth place."

Through his volunteer work with the girl's AAU team and his association with other volunteer organizations such as Special Olympics, Marvin and Mary Lou have seen what he describes as "The most powerful force in our country—people freely giving their resources expecting in return the satisfaction of seeing others find success."

They use Robert Tiedge, a supporter of his AAU teams, as an example. "One of the most difficult problems you encounter in amateur basketball is finding enough money for uniforms, lodging, and so on," explains Mary Lou. "Short of door-to-door fund raising we really didn't know how we'd be able to get money. During the first year Digger was very generous. Later, a former neighbor of his, Bob Tiedge, gave us a call. He said that he'd normally sponsored Karen Phelp's softball team each summer and that he'd heard that Karen would not be playing because of her commitment to AAU basketball. He wanted to know more about the program. Marvin invited him to attend a practice game. Bob came and afterwards offered to buy the team dinner. Before they ate Marvin asked one of the girls to give God thanks for the meal. Bob must have been impressed with what he saw because he offered to pay for the girls rooms and meals for the team's trip downstate—this was a gift from God because we did not know how we were going to get the money to pay for those things. Bob has continued in his support for AAU for over ten years now."

"He's been involved in finding girls to play, arranging places for us to play, and planning trips," says Marvin. "He once told me that his father had told him it didn't matter how much money you made—if you didn't share some of it you could never really enjoy it. Well, I've watched Bob and others like him share their time, energy, and money. If you were to ask them if its worth it, I'm certain their answer would be 'yes.' That's the great thing about giving something precious away—doing so seems to double the value—both the giver and receiver get something from the transaction."

Marvin coached girls' AAU teams for seven years and won a national championship in 1988. His coaching abilities impressed one of his young players so much that she told her college athletic director they ought to hire him as a head coach—which was exactly what Jo-Ann Nester at St. Mary's University in South Bend did.

"When I came here in 1984 one of my first responsibilities was to find a head basketball coach." says Jo-Ann, "Tammy Radke, one of our better players, mentioned Marvin. I asked him if he was interested. He said he was and sent me a resume. When I checked his references all I heard was praise—I hired him and he's proven to be the best thing to ever happen to basketball here at St. Mary's.

"He struggled in his first season. I think the girls were 4-14 that year—but within a year he completely changed the direction of this program. He's had winning seasons ever since. In fact, in his third year we got an invitation to play in the NAIA post-season tournament and have now graduated from that division into the NCAA Division III. Normally, you would expect to struggle for a year or two in a higher division, but our girls have continued to win. Marvin has had a lot to do with their success . . . He teaches basketball, he's patient and its not his style to put his team out on the floor without first getting them prepared to play . . . He has his own set of standards and he refuses to compromise. Fortunately, his standards and mine are quite similar. In short, Marvin is an athletic director's dream."

Jo-Ann adds that she tries to find coaches to act as role models for the young women in St. Mary's various sports programs. "I look for coaches who can win—but, more importantly, I look for role models for our young women. Generally speaking the best role models are successful women. Even so, there's no doubt in my mind that Marvin is the best role model for the young ladies in our basketball program."

Wood has enjoyed his seven years at St. Mary's. "Its been a great situation," he admits. "They've been understanding about my commitments to my job at the high school. I don't get a lot of interference from parents or the administration. Aside from the standards I set for myself and the team, there's no pressure." Marvin adds that he enjoys the challenge of developing a college program. "I've especially enjoyed the challenge of recruiting. St. Mary's does not offer scholarships, but the university and the area make an attractive package for young women who want to get an education at a small school noted for its academic excellence."

"I'm amazed at all of the contacts he's developed," says Jo-Ann. "He has people from all over calling him about young women. Over the last couple of years he's brought several talented gals into the program. In many cases I believe they come here because they want to play for Marvin."

* *

During the Spring of each year following the 1954 state championship, the Milan basketball team has held a reunion. Marvin and Mary Lou held the first one at their residence in New Castle and through the years the event has moved from

Milan to Indianapolis to Mishawaka. These reunions have provided Marvin and Mary Lou with a wealth of fond memories. They've watched the members of the team grow and become successful. "Its been great to be a part of their lives," says Marvin. "We've been to their weddings, rejoiced at the birth of their children and shared both their success and sorrow. They've all become a part of our family."

Each member of the '54 team has gone on to find success in their lives after the championship season. Bobby Plump played ball at Butler and then went on to star as a player and coach for Phillips Petroleum's professional basketball team. Since getting out of basketball, Bobby has developed a successful financial planning business in Indianapolis. Ray Craft, who also went to Butler, became a coach, teacher, and, later, a principal at Shelbyville High School. Ray is currently Assistant Commissioner of the IHSAA.

Gene White, Ronnie Truitt, Rollin Cutter, Glenn Butte (Butte played college basketball at Indiana University) and Roger Schroeder also followed in Marvin's footsteps as teachers and coaches. In fact, Gene White later coached at Milan. Bill Jordan has found success on the stage and on the silver screen and Bob Engel has had a long and successful career in the automobile industry. Bob Wichman attended Purdue University and became an executive for the Pioneer Seed Company. Ken Wendleman and Ken Delap stayed in Ripley County.

In 1988 members of the '54 team mourned the death of Ronnie Truitt, who died after a bout with cancer. Truitt, who made his home in Texas after graduating from the University of Houston, had a school named after him in honor of his years of dedicated service to education in his community.

Of all the many get-togethers and reunions, the 1985 reunion was especially memorable. Earlier that year, Indiana natives Angelo Pizzo and David Anspaugh announced their intention to produce a movie loosely based upon the '54 Milan Indians.

"The movie was a big topic at that reunion," recalls Marvin. "It seemed like almost every year something about Milan had been brought up during the state tournament. When we'd get together we'd talk about such things. But the idea that someone was interested in making a movie based on that team, well, that floored us ... We speculated on what the film might be like and we hoped it would be representative of what had happened way back then."

Pizzo and Anspaugh chose Indiana as the site for shooting the film which would star Gene Hackman, Dennis Hopper, and Barbara Hershey. Other roles were filled by Hoosiers. Ray Craft, by then the assistant commissioner of the IHSAA, played a similar role in the film.

Pizzo and Anspaugh were quick to explain that the movie was not the Milan story. "Hoosiers," they explained, would be a film about second chances. And, indeed the film was not at all like the Milan story. For example, the coach, played by Gene Hackman, was a temperamental sort who more closely resembled the frenzied Bobby Knight than the composed Marvin Wood.

Pizzo asked Marvin to be a technical advisor, but Marvin declined. "It was tough to turn down," says Marvin. "Given different circumstances I would have liked to be a part of it. Doing so, however, probably would have required me to give up the coaching position at St. Mary's and I would have had to take an extended leave from my counseling position at Mishawaka. Besides, the movie they were planning to make was not the Milan story—there were quite a few differences . . . I don't mean this in a cocky way, but I'd already had a front row seat to the real thing and I didn't see how it could be any better than that. In the end what made up my mind [not to do it] was the fact that I was still involved in coaching competitive basketball and I preferred that over helping with the movie."

When the movie came out in November of 1986 Marvin and Mary Lou attended its premiere showing at the Circle Theater in Indianapolis. "I enjoyed the movie," says Marvin. "Even though it was not the Milan story it was related to what really happened at Milan. I liked the theme about second chances. Few people make it through life without stumbling along the way and we all deserve that second chance. I thought the film accurately portrayed the small-town spirit of the game. And, most importantly, it was a family-oriented film."

"The movie has brought us quite a bit of publicity," adds Mary Lou. "We've received many letters since its been out and much of it has not just been from Indiana. We've heard from people all over the country."

Marvin laughingly adds that he would like to make it clear that he's never hit one of his players, nor is his temperament anything like that of the character played by Gene Hackman. "I'm no Norman Dale," he confesses. "In all the years I've coached I don't think I've been given more than a total of twenty technical fouls. I've always believed that the coach who's ranting and raving at the refs isn't paying attention to what's happening in the game. Maybe some coaches can get away with giving up that edge, but I never could. I have all I can handle in concentrating on my own team's play."

"Hoosiers" became a box office hit, further enhancing the image of Indiana as a basketball state and renewing the memories of Milan's championship, which was now over thirty years old. In 1987 the Woods were invited to New York city to a dinner given by John Brademus in honor of: "Indiana natives who have distinguished themselves as excellent examples of Hoosiers." At Mary Lou's insistence, Marvin took time away from his coaching and counseling to make the trip to New York.

"Pizzo and Anspaugh were the honored guests at that dinner," Mary Lou recalls. "We met Howard Cosell and his wife, Kurt Vonnegut, and Jane Pauley who was also born in Morristown. Marvin gave a short speech in which he thanked David and Angelo for making a film based upon the '54 team. That night was probably the second most exciting evening in my life."

"We found out that all of those people are still basketball fans at heart," adds Marvin. "I can't imagine another state in the union where a gathering of its distinguished citizenry would include a high school basketball coach. I was honored to be there and became even more aware of the fact that basketball is an important part of our Hoosier heritage."

Mr. and Mrs. Howard Cosell with Marvin and Mary Lou Wood at a dinner hosted by Dr. John Brademus. (Courtesy NYU/Phil Berkun)

Marvin poses with fellow Hoosiers. Left to right: Angelo Pizzo, David Anspaugh, Jane Pauley and John Brademus. (Courtesy NYU/Phil Berkun)

The Spring of 1989 found Marvin anxiously anticipating his retirement. Nearly forty years had passed since he'd opened his first basketball practice in a tiny gym at French Lick. Now, at age sixty three, he looked forward to the new challenges retirement would bring. Specifically, he'd set his eye on the political arena where he felt he might bring a fresh perspective into state politics. "I've always voted and I've always been interested in the political process," he explains. "But as a basketball coach you can't get involved in party politics because of the obvious conflicts it would inevitably cause. In fact, where ever we've lived Mary Lou has always registered as a Republican and I a Democrat. But privately I've always been fascinated by politics and I've spent a lot of time deciding exactly where I stand on political issues."

"When I got out of coaching at the high school level I did get involved as a campaign manager and I enjoyed the experience. As I looked down the road at retirement, if I had to decide on one thing that I might like to do—it would be to run for public office."

Ironically, about the same time Marvin was thinking about getting into politics, the Republican party was considering him as a potential candidate. "Late in the Spring of 1989 I went down to Indianapolis to receive special recognition from the legislature. After meeting with the legislature, Dick Mangus [a state legislator] asked me if I'd come to a meeting with the state nominating committee. At that meeting they asked me if I'd think about running for the fifth district state representative as a Republican." Marvin expressed his interest, explaining that he'd been a Democrat for most of his life, but would have no qualms about switching parties.

"I didn't have a problem with switching parties. Most members of my family are Democrats and in our political discussions over the years I began to discover that my opinions were somewhat contrary to theirs. The older I grew the more I began to realize that my political opinions had shifted right of the Democratic party. Running as a Republican was not a problem. I did have concerns about getting organized and raising money, but within a few months the party convinced me that I would be able to raise enough money. They promised to help along the way. In August 1989 I announced my intention to run for fifth district state representative.

"When my relatives learned I'd be running as a Republican they gave me a lot of grief, but I'm sure they meant no harm. In fact, when one of my cousins found out she sent us a letter which read: 'Your grandfather swore the only Republican he'd ever vote for was Irv Duerkson (an Illinois senator)—but now I believe there are two.'"

Shortly after Marvin announced his intention to run, his opponent, Craig Fry, accused him of making a "back room" deal with the Republican party. "This surprised me," says Marvin. "He [Fry] knew darn well a deal had been offered, but that offer came from a Democrat." Marvin never made the details of that offer public. "Win or lose I wanted voters to see me as a positive candidate," he explains. "I didn't think the political advantage I might have been able to gain would be worth the cost to my self-esteem."

In October of 1989 Marvin went to Washington with a group of Republicans from around the country to meet with President George Bush and Vice-President Dan Quayle. "He came home from that trip about as excited as I've ever seen him," remembers Mary Lou. "When he got home he told me he now realized that he'd been a Republican for a long time."

"I enjoyed meeting George Bush and Dan Quayle," says Marvin. "But beyond that I was impressed with the ideas I heard from fellow Republicans from around the country. It was nothing at all like we're sometimes led to believe. These people are concerned about domestic problems, about poverty, unemployment, and the environment. If I learned anything at all from that trip it was that the Republican party is not a party for the wealthy or a few special interest groups. Republicans are interested in good government, and so am I."

By January of 1990 Marvin found a campaign manager and organized the various committees needed to conduct the campaign. The state organization, "Victory 90," promised funds and organizational assistance and Marvin spent an ever-increasing amount of time reviewing a strategy for victory. "We knew we had an uphill battle," he recalls. "We were inexperienced and the district had been targeted by both parties as a 'must-win' district. Our opponent had an established organization and a lot of union money. On the other hand, we were counting on volunteers and the generosity of individuals."

"The fifth district is a difficult district to win for either party," adds Robert Tanguy who was assigned by "Victory 90" to help coordinate Marvin's campaign. "It covers a lot of area and consists of a wide range of neighborhoods. In Elkhart county, for example, the fifth district includes both some of the poorest and some of the richest neighborhoods. Another problem is that the area is in a major media market. This means radio and television spots are not cheap. We knew Fry would get a bundle of union money and we were going to have to find a way to raise a similar sum. We thought we had a good chance to win, but it was going to be a tough fight."

As Marvin began to realize the magnitude of the task in front of him he spent even more time on his campaign. His work day now included eight hours at the high school, a two hour practice or game at St. Mary's and as many extra hours as he could find to work on the campaign.

"During one stretch in February he went twenty-one straight days with less than six hours of sleep," confides Mary Lou. "He'd be up each morning by six and many times he'd not go to bed until well after midnight."

The rigorous schedule Marvin set for himself quickly began to take its toll. By the end of February he began to feel weak and experienced some health problems. Then, late one evening after putting in a full twelve hour day, he started to retire for the night when he discovered a lump on the side of his neck. "It was one of those nights when he'd been working to get things organized," Mary Lou recalls. "He'd been putting too much pressure on himself and we were a little frustrated right then because we weren't really certain as to how we were going to accomplish some of the things we needed to do. Anyway, we'd been talking about raising money or something and Marvin was so worn out I told him he ought to go to bed and forget about the campaign for one night. He went upstairs then came back down and showed me this big lump he'd found on his neck." Marvin went to the doctor the next day and even before the examination was finished he could sense the news was not good.

"After you've been a counselor for a few years you can begin to read body language and I could tell by the way Doctor Reed was reacting that something was definitely wrong. He said that he had a pretty good idea as to what had caused the lump, and recommended I see a surgeon to have it biopsied. We scheduled the appointment for the next day and by the end of the week we discovered I had cancer."

In the days and weeks that followed, Marvin put the campaign, coaching, and counseling behind him. He was now confronted with the biggest challenge of his life---he had to face his own mortality.

"When the doctor told me I had cancer my initial response was to think: 'I've worked forty years and just as I get ready to retire I have to face this.' I experienced feelings of bitterness. But then, as I thought more about my life and began to look back at all the great memories, I was reminded that I've had a great life. And, as I sat there wondering if I'd spent my last Christmas with my family, my emotions soon turned from bitterness to one of quiet resolve. I prayed to God to give me the strength to handle all that lay before me and I thanked him for the wonderful life he gave me."

Mary Lou, too, found comfort in prayer and her relationship with God. "Without prayer and a belief in a higher power, I would not have been able to handle this situation," she confesses. "I needed a powerful crutch to help me. I prayed that God would have His will and then tried to have confidence in the professionals to whom we turned for help."

Marvin turned to oncologist Dr. Rafat Ansari, who diagnosed his cancer as lymphatic lymphoma. The disease, he was told, had not spread to his other organs. They'd detected it at a fairly early stage thus it could be treated. In late March

Marvin travelled to the University of Chicago to get a second opinion. The doctors there concurred with Dr. Ansari's diagnosis and recommended that Marvin be treated at home. Within three weeks of detection, Marvin was placed on a regimen that would attempt to put the disease into remission. His treatment involved the use of chemotherapy in a series of increasing doses. Marvin was told to drink plenty of water and to eat regular, sensible meals. His doctors explained that the treatment worked by washing the cancer out of the body through the urinary system.

He was also informed that the chemotherapy would leave him without hair and that during the latter treatments, as his white blood cell count went lower, he would become increasingly susceptible to viruses. His doctor advised him to continue with all of his normal activities, but cautioned him against becoming run down.

While the first news of cancer had been a devastating blow, the subsequent information of the extent and the possibility of recovery did much to buoy the Woods' spirits. "That first night we found out Marvin had cancer was the worst night of my life," Mary Lou recalls. "But as we got into the process and discovered there was still plenty to hope for, I felt a little better. I told Marvin when they discovered the cancer had not spread to other organs that I considered that a sectional championship; and then when they told us it could be treated—that was a regional championship. I figured if he responded well to the treatment I'd consider that a semi-state championship; and if he could get it into remission, it would be a state championship."

News of Marvin's cancer quickly spread throughout the state and in no time he was deluged by mail and phone calls from fans, friends, and former players. "I found out people really do care," says Wood. "But I also discovered that the 'C' word frightens the heck out of people. I had friends who would do anything to avoid mentioning it. I think some people had already written me off. People don't seem to realize that you can come back from cancer. You can beat it. You can live---this was the message in a lot of the letters I received from people who'd had cancer. The letters from those folks were especially gratifying because they gave me hope.

"I can't say that the days and weeks during my treatment were easy. And I don't think anyone could have adequately prepared me for those chemo treatments. Even so, the doctors and nurses involved in giving the treatments were great. They answered all of my questions and they were always positive... It seemed as though when things got really rough, on those days when I was feeling low, someone beautiful always seemed to step into my life. One such special person was Jenine Plump. She'd been through a bout with cancer herself and she and Bobby called every week. They knew what I was going through and constantly reassured me that I would indeed get better."

As Wood began his treatment, he faced a difficult decision. He had to decide whether or not to continue his campaign for fifth district state representative. "My first thought was that my health was far more important than the campaign," says Marvin. "I asked Doctor Ansari if he thought it would be wise for me to continue the campaign and he encouraged me to continue with my activities just as I would had I not had cancer. Despite his reassurances I still had misgivings about continuing to run. I knew I would be losing my hair, which would make public appearances a little awkward. I was worried about having enough energy to wage a successful campaign and I wondered if the Republican party would still want me to run. Most importantly, Mary Lou did not want me to get too run down, further jeopardizing my health.

"I had several discussions with Keith Bulen and Bob Tanguy about these things and had all but made my up mind not to run. In fact, I had planned a trip to New Castle to do a recording about Milan for the Hall of Fame and made plans to meet with Keith and Bob to tell them I would not be running."

Retired Brigadier General Bob Tanguy, who helped to coordinate the Wood campaign, recalls that meeting. "When we first heard about the cancer we were all holding our breath. Marvin is not only a special person, but a state treasure as well and when we do lose him it will be a sad day indeed. We were heartened to hear the news that the cancer was treatable. Marvin and I talked a little about what he might do about the campaign and I knew he was leaning towards quitting. So, when he came down to Indianapolis and told me he thought he ought to withdraw I was not too surprised. But knowing as much as I did about cancer I told him that if his doctor said it was all right to continue then he ought to think about going ahead with the campaign. We talked about it some more and then I asked him to come back to see Keith Bulen and me after he got done at the Hall of Fame. I told him that the three of us needed to have a skull session.

"The next day at 2:00 Marvin came back in. Keith Bulen and Marvin and I got in a room and Bulen said: 'Look Marvin, I'm in here running this thing without any pecuniary compensation.' Then he opened up his pill box and, as only Keith Bulen can do, he showed Marvin the five or six different medications he has to take for his heart, for his lungs, and so forth. 'You see all of those pills?' he says. 'I'm taking them regularily and I'm still probably going to die a hell-of-a-lot sooner than you are.' Bulen and I told him that he's an inspiration to tens of thousands of people and he became such an inspiration because he's a fighter. We told him that we'd never heard of him throwing in the towel before and that now was a damn poor time to start doing it.

"I told him that the greatest medicine in the world was a mind at work. I told him that if he quit this race and went off somewhere to worry about this cancer business he was going to be the most miserable guy in the world and he'd probably end up dying—'its going to get you,' I said. 'But if you're out there fighting Fry and the Democrat ticket you're going to be so busy that you'll keep the cancer thing in the proper perspective.' And to this day, I firmly believe that to be the truth.

"When we were finished he stood up from his seat and said, 'You guys have really lit up my Christmas tree. Let me go home and talk to Mary Lou and I'll give you answer in the morning.' By the time we finished our meeting the guy who went charging out of that office was completely different than the one who'd come in."

Marvin called them the next day and let them know he was back in the race. "When I went down to tell them I was withdrawing I thought I was doing what was best for all the parties involved," explains Marvin. "I figured they would find a younger candidate with more energy, time and good health to replace me. When I discovered they were still interested in seeing me run, I began to reconsider my decision. The other thing that convinced me to stay in was the fact they agreed with my priorities which were my health, my family, and then the campaign."

With these priorities in mind, Marvin spent the Summer of 1990 performing a delicate balancing act between conducting a political campaign and battling lymphatic cancer. "Victory 90" gave as much help as they could, even so, Marvin continued to lag behind his opponent in polls. The news of his cancer had hurt his chances as many voters assumed the worst.

While the campaign lagged in the polls, Marvin's body responded well to the chemotherapy. In early July a Cat Scan showed the tumor had been reduced by about eight times its original size. Marvin's blood counts continued to improve and with only three treatments remaining Marvin and Mary Lou had plenty of reason for optimism.

Then in August Marvin's health took a turn for the worst. While working the booth for the Cancer Society during "sidewalk days" in Mishawaka, Marvin got caught in a rainstorm which caused him to catch a cold. Under normal conditions the immune system has little difficulty in ridding the body of a cold virus, but Marvin's immune system, decimated by the chemotherapy treatments, was not strong enough to fight the virus.

Marvin's temperature shot up to one hundred and one and shortly thereafter he found himself in a hospital bed fighting for his life. Unable to get his temperature down, his doctors brought in a infection specialist to see what, if any, antibiotic could rid Marvin of the virus. "He prescribed several antibiotics which didn't do much good," recalls Mary Lou. "As they tried to find something to help his body combat the virus, I feared that his fevers would eventually weaken him to the point where he'd not be able to overcome neither the virus nor the cancer."

Fortunately, Mary Lou's worst fears did not come to pass. Little by little Marvin's white blood cell count rose and by his third day in the hospital his immune system began to attack the virus with a vengeance. "Once, while they were changing antibiotics for about the third time, I asked my doctor what kind of treatment they were giving me," smiles Marvin. "He told me they were giving me the 'SWAG' treatment. When I asked him what that meant he said: 'Scientific-Wild-Ass-Guess.' He then assured me that as my blood count improved I was going to get better no matter what they gave me. And, thank God, he was right."

Marvin was out of the hospital within a week. They'd hoped to keep the fact that he'd been in the hospital as quiet as possible, but his political opponent found out about the stay and tried to gain from it by suggesting the Republicans were continuing to run a candidate who quite probably would not be alive to take the office for which he was running. The Wood campaign tried to rebut this assertion in a press conference with

Marvin's doctors. Despite their assurances that Marvin would indeed be around to take office should he win, the Wood campaign fell further behind in the polls.

During the months of September and October the Marvin and his army of volunteers stepped up their efforts to overcome Fry's seven to ten point lead. On the strength of a spirited-effort they were able to overcome that gap by the first week in October. For his part, Marvin was everywhere. Speaking to as many as five gatherings a day, he hustled all over the district. "I figured it was the least I could do given all the support I was receiving. If not for the efforts of volunteers we would have been even further behind and would have had little chance of catching up.

"I cannot find the words to express my gratitude for all the people who gave their time, energy, and money. One Saturday in Elkhart County, for example, we had seventy-five people show up to go door-to-door with us. On another occasion we had at least fifty people show up in Mishawaka to do the same kind of thing."

Early October was full of good news for Marvin and Mary Lou. Most polls showed the race to be dead even—and, more importantly, Wood's doctors were able to assure him that his cancer was in complete remission. "You cannot imagine what a relief it was to hear that the cancer was in remission," says Mary Lou. "I'd tried so hard not to worry about it, turned it over to God and the doctors as best I could, but there were times when I wondered, times when I worried. And to hear that beautiful word from the doctor—'remission'—I'd said that when we knew the cancer had been put in remission we'd count it as a state championship, but it's much sweeter than that."

"The experience has made me confront my own mortality," adds Marvin. "As a result of the cancer, I've had to re-evaluate my priorities in regard to my relationships with God, with my family, and with what I'd been planning to do with the rest of my life. I'm pleased with the plans I've made for the rest of my days. I say this without any arrogance—I've had a good life, and while I'm not ready to die I'm comfortable with my relationship with God and I'm ready to go whenever he should see fit to take me."

Wood adds that he thinks the keys to his success in battling the disease were detecting it early, employing the best doctors available, following the prescribed treatment, praying daily, and, perhaps most importantly, maintaining a positive attitude. "With all of the modern technology available, you can recover from cancer," Wood is emphatic on this point. "Where there is hope and a will to survive there can be success. I was fortunate in that I was surrounded by people with positive attitudes—they were full of hope and hope is contagious."

Marvin's doctors told him he could continue to live a normal lifestyle and should be periodically examined to make certain the cancer remains in remission.

With the battle against cancer behind him, Marvin pushed on in his campaign with renewed enthusiasm. As election day drew closer, however, he knew he had an uphill battle. "The cancer did a lot to set us back, but we had other problems too. We were inexperienced and as the final weeks of the campaign passed I felt our inexperience caught up with us. We had communication and organization problems between us and the people in Indianapolis. On many occasions it seemed to me that the left hand didn't know what the right hand was doing. I didn't know how to solve that problem. In the meantime, our opponent appeared to be well organized and he was attacking us right and left."

Marvin and Mary Lou spent election night at the Republican party headquarters watching the early returns. Fry maintained a modest lead throughout the night. As midnight approached a software problem in Elkhart County slowed that County's returns to a trickle. Officials said it would be hours before the results would be available. The Wood campaign counted heavily on Elkhart County votes to win and, trailing by about two hundred votes in St. Joseph County, Marvin and Mary Lou went to bed that night not knowing if they'd won or lost. "Yes, despite being worn out from a hectic day, it was still difficult to fall asleep that night," admits Marvin. "I figured we'd lost and my heart was heavy for all of the people who'd given so much to get me elected."

In the morning Marvin's suspicions were confirmed—the unofficial tally had Craig Fry winning by seventy-five votes. By the early evening the margin was further reduced to just thirty-five votes. Such a narrow defeat prompted the Republican party to request a recount to which Marvin reluctantly agreed. "I didn't want to look like I was complaining about the results or crying foul-play," explains Marvin. "And at the same time I felt like the party and my supporters deserved to have any chance at a victory."

Weeks later a recount commission confirmed Fry's victory—by a mere twenty-five votes—thus ending Marvin's first political campaign in defeat. "It just wasn't meant to be," muses Mary Lou. "But, given the fact that Marvin was going to live, the election loss was not that difficult for us to take. We were a lot more disappointed for our supporters than we were for ourselves."

"It was a great experience," adds Marvin. "We met a lot of nice people and I learned a lot about politics... In politics—like that old adage about love and war—anything goes." Concerning future political ambitions, Marvin does not see himself in the role of a politician. "To achieve the kind of success I would expect of myself I would have to make too many compromises. I've built my reputation on being both an honest man and a positive influence. To tarnish that reputation in the pursuit of some political end would be a mistake."

Epilogue

On a sunny March afternoon in the Hoosier Dome, Marvin Wood sits with Mary Lou and a host of friends around him. Many months have passed since his last chemotherapy and he's regained a few pounds and most of the rim of gray hair which surrounds the barren top of his head. He appears to be more relaxed than he'd been during those hectic months from the previous year and has retained a bit of color from a Christmas trip to Florida where he and Mary Lou spent time with their daughter, son-in-law, and grandchildren.

On the floor below him, tiny Whitko high school battles Gary Roosevelt for an opportunity to play for the state championship in the evening. As would seem appropriate Marvin and Mary Lou are rooting for the underdog. Mary Lou is not quite as vociferous as she was thirty seven years ago, but the more vocal of the two nonetheless. Earlier in the week they attended the Hall of Fame banquet where Ray Craft became the third member of the '54 Milan team to be inducted in the the Indiana Basketball Hall of Fame.

During a break in the action, a couple of young men slip into Marvin's row and ask him for an autograph. Marvin and Mary Lou have been attending state basketball finals for almost every year after the Milan championship and every year Marvin signs at least a dozen autographs. "I can't believe people still remember," he laughs. "Those boys told me that I was responsible for keeping class basketball out of Indiana. I don't really believe that to be true, but it thrills me to see young men and women with a sense of the history of the game."

As Wood surveys the Hoosier Dome filled with thirty-thousand-or-so spectators, he feels a sense of pride in the fact that he has been able to play a role in such a successful tradition. "State Championship weekend is always a special time for us," he admits. "We see so many folks here who have had their day out there [he points to the playing floor] and over the years we've all become like one big, happy family. I guess you can say that State Championship weekend is like a family reunion and every year we add a new teams and new people to the family."

When asked what he's doing in his retirement, Marvin begins by ticking off the names of the recruits he's trying to get for his St. Mary's team. Mary Lou shakes her head and laughs as she listens to him. "I don't expect he'll ever give up coaching," she smiles. "I used to think that as we got older and both retired the most involvement we'd have with basketball would be as spectators. But when I watch him instructing the girls and I see the intent look or their faces I realize that Marvin still has something to give to the game. He enjoys it and I believe as long as there's a team out there that will have him—Marvin will be coaching."

Author's Note

Unfortunately, at the time this book went to press Marvin Wood's cancer has recurred. The recurrence was caught at an early stage and this time Marvin is "going for the cure" rather than remission. He and Mary Lou would appreciate your prayers.